THE TIES THAT BIND

T.C. MONK

Published 2023

Print ISBN: 9798223944539

First Edition

57,753 total words

Other Works by the Author

– Poetry –
∴

Imperfections of Beauty

=

Beautiful Imperfections
[Book 2]

– Sci-fi –
∴

Lumen's Quiddity
{'Pariah' series}

=

Daedal Convergence
{Book 2}

=

Orphic Dénouement
[Book 3 - Due out late 2027]

– Prison/Nonfiction –
∴

T.O.M.B.
(Those of My Blood)

– Fiction –
∴

Velvet Smoke

=

Beyond The Veil

– Erotica –
∴

Masculine Shadows

Dedication

This creation is dedicated to all those seeking a more profound enlightenment about matters that affect their lives. Its purpose is not only for those who tirelessly pursue the truth but also for anyone who works diligently to deepen the knowledge they seek to enhance their lives. It is more difficult than some might realize to step out and forge one's own path toward changing one's personal philosophy, as such a goal can be daunting for those afraid of change. Nonetheless, I have created this entire collection of educational writings for these individuals, offering it so others can learn to change their thinking—by their own effort—and for those eager to explore self-discovery.

I am also dedicating this entire work to the creation of Life. I am humbled by the countless ways it reveals itself to each person, whether alone or together, and by its relentless drive for growth that pushes us all forward.

Contents

Introduction

'Welcome to my Mind!'

I cannot help but feel a bit vulnerable writing this, as it is the first time I am allowing others to consider and assess my thoughts with autonomy. Such a concession is not an easily digestible concept; however, I am confident enough to lay bare my refined intellect as I guide each reader through the pages of The Ties That Bind. This production is geared toward those seeking to refine the contrived influences shaping human reality and is the sole creation of this author - unless otherwise noted.

In constructing this detailed Opus, I aimed to avoid delving into the fundamental valuations these notions are known to harbor while introducing my interpretation of each to the curious mind. My purpose was to present these individual concepts in a more cultured manner, so that a more profound definition of these themes could bring further refinement to one's Life. Its complement is not intended to dismantle, detract, or supplant what has already been established regarding each subject rendered herein, but to serve as an addendum to the currently established principle ascribed to each and to proffer an alternate perspective on them. Designing it in this manner was not only meant to bring clarity to the reader—a measure for one to further consider the details regarding each subject matter—but also to reveal how all of our lives are connected by The Ties That Bind. Its details were also included to show how they directly affect perceived reality, each based on one's various points of compromise and relative assimilation.

When I embarked on the quest for self-enlightenment, I realized that most of my knowledge was a mishmash of flawed concepts drawn from various subjective sources. These notions not only contradicted what was commonly accepted but had become a harmful malignancy in my mind. My desire was not only to refine my thoughts and bring them into balance, but also to share a measure of clarity with those longing for erudite learning and with anyone struggling with similar, conflicting ideas. As intimated above, such a shortcoming is not only personal and difficult to expose but also necessary to demonstrate the authenticity of truth in revelation.

The accumulation of knowledge - and its comprehension - has been an insatiable passion of mine since I began this journey. As I began work on this manuscript, I had no idea what to expect, what this creation would become, or how it would ultimately affect my life. I became enamored with collecting it and with how it can promote progressive thinking among those seeking its verity. With due diligence and a relentless yearning to succeed, the objectives one pursues in life will be revealed by one's will to attain them. Looking back now, it is humbling to realize that, whatever my initial thoughts were, it has completely surpassed all my expectations.

As I embarked on this creative project, I aimed not only to uncover the mysteries within each concept but also to help others gain a deeper understanding of how design is created, both proactively and reactively. This symbiosis is evident in the dynamic relationship between what I proffer for consumption and what nurtures the desire to learn. This is further evidenced in the title of this work, which is representative of and rooted in what not only links these treatises together but also reveals their genuine concentric nature.

Initially, my ambition for this compilation was to script it as an exclusive piece of scholarly nonfiction—a pedagogical narrative—and not to cloud it with personal commentary. I wished to be taken seriously as an academic, one of the literati. However, I was persuaded otherwise by a group of folks who were offered a chance to review and critique the original draft in its infancy and were kind enough to pass along notes for revision and correction. This clique of individuals was faculty and student interns of "The Pen Project' classes taught in the School of Humanities, Arts, and Cultural Studies at Arizona State University's West Campus. In several pieces of feedback, participants suggested adding a personal touch to the articles to strengthen their overall feel and reception, making them more personable and enabling readers to connect with the author on a deeper level.

None of the responses to these submissions were overly critical, but they were poignant and analytical. I learned from them and thus modified my writing to be more cohesive and receptive to the reader. Three particular statements in the feedback actually humbled me. The first, from Rose, a Pen Project Intern in Spring 2021, read, "Your writing reminds me of Emerson's." The second, from Isabelle Noel, a Pen Project Intern in Spring 2021, read, "As I read your composition, I was reminded of the writing and rhetoric of ancient philosophers like Aristotle, Socrates, and Descartes." The third, from Raven, a Pen Project Intern in Fall 2021, reads, "All I can say is wow, wow, WOW! This piece has come out amazing, and although I once had a hard time in philosophy and ethics class in college, this is the first time I have been completely interested in this field." Such tremendous plaudits from other human beings. I was at a loss for words, yet humbled and proud to be mentioned alongside some immortal masters.

Despite the ego stroking, I did not let it cloud my judgment. I took some of their advice and began reshaping and retooling these pieces of artistic expression, acting after allotting myself a significant amount of Time to reflect on what I wished to modify. It was essential to gain a thorough and nuanced understanding of one's own knowledge and beliefs before sharing them with the world. The reason for this was twofold: First, to refrain from imparting incorrect, unsound, or faulty theories to the reader. Second, I wanted to clarify this for myself and my intended audience by drawing attention to what may lie beneath the surface of existence.

Now, in a general sense, most people may already be conversant with the broad subject matter contained in this labor; however, I implore each reader to refrain from making any prejudgments without at least scanning the plethora of information contained herein. The sheer scope of knowledge in this body of work is intense and intended to be thought-provoking, eliciting an emotional response in those who consume it. In designing this manuscript, I was careful to avoid incorporating references to evangelicalism. My intention was not to script it with any religious undertones, but rather to shape it from a place of neutrality, free from imperious influences—those contrived with specific intent and purpose that fall outside the realm of altruistic teaching.

Please do not assume I am banging against any Faith-based practices, groups, or specific doctrines, as I am not. Religion (in this author's opinion) has enough influence in the world without needing to be mentioned in this work, nor did I wish to lend support from its authority to lend weight and credibility to a standalone creation. For one to contrive an artificial thread of pious connection between their work and the reader could be interpreted as an intentional attempt to prey upon one's devotional tenets (things held sacred to each person), which I want no part of.

I would ask the reader to consider this work a collection of my thoughts on each subject, to help others achieve greater transparency in their lives. The position I cite here not only addresses how anyone may struggle with such concepts and why they are battling them, but also clarifies why such conflicts exist and establishes a causal connection between my ink pen and their brain. It is no small feat to touch another person from a distance and leave a lasting image of beauty in their mind's eye. Such has been my ambition for quite some time. With this production, I now have the opportunity to seek out that connection, establish it, and help build something that can benefit another's existence.

Scripting this work in the manner I have, in effect, allows me to incorporate my thoughts into the lives of my readers. Such an endeavor provides them with something to ponder, not only for the benevolent purposes it may yield, but also to share a measure of my Life with those beyond this haze-filled hutch that keeps me captive. However, in doing so, I was not prepared for the level of detail required for each topic or how deeply I would need to look beneath its veneer to achieve such clarity. It was quite a burdensome task to execute.

I ask each reader to keep in mind that this production is not intended for casual reading but rather to prompt the audience to proactively enhance their core knowledge. With this in mind, I created brief title introductions for each article to establish a baseline definition and frame its complement for better comprehension. Crafting it in this style had dual motives: first, to clarify its purpose; and second, to give those who consume its product a chance to expand their knowledge beyond what they currently possess.

That said, allow me to elucidate what I mean by 'not for light or easy reading.'

According to those who have established the boundaries of consummate knowledge, there is an undeniable commingling of forces converging far and wide, which are imperative for creation to exist as it is perceived. All things in existence are based on bipartisanship with some other form of Life. The seminal association between these diverse entities lies in the substance that sustains them and in how they continue to develop and expand throughout the known universe.

The product I refer to is, in essence, more codependent than autonomous. It must exist in such a state, as nothing in known creation is independent of its constitution, especially if it is alive. This blending of materials is the proverbial formula for how each substance propagates and is maintained. Take the quiddity of a star, for instance; from the solar winds its fires produce, down to its core, everything it is feeds another part of its corporeal essence. And, like the human body, which functions much the same way, it, too, will one day burn out.

There is a common thread in all that exists, and it is essential to progress in one form or another. However, when it comes to the pattern of Life design, everything one engages in should support its promotion. Life was not meant to remain idle or be resolved by contentment, but rather to be pursued through the achievements one can dream of, hunt for, or spend one's entire Life toiling to attain what one desires most.

Our species is the most novel creation in our known universe. Humans are what they covet and what they despise, all in the same breath. This creates an incredible dichotomy of Love and Hate like no other. Why such a division exists among our species is an enigma, despite its existence since Time immemorial. Despite humans sometimes exhibiting such antipathy toward one another, this author hopes that humanity can grow beyond the aforementioned petty trivialities and focus more on its intellect, becoming more tolerant and resilient than ever.

In constructing this Opus, I incorporated specific nouns, adjectives, and pronoun forms to enhance clarity for the reader. This referred not only to our species as a whole but also to the individual, regardless of where each word appears in the text. I have also deliberately chosen to capitalize specific keywords throughout this creation for two reasons. #1) To direct readers' attention to a particular section of this manuscript where the corresponding definition can be found. For page identification, each keyword can be located in the 'Table of Contents.' #2) To demonstrate how these terms relate, creating 'The Ties That Bind' us all together.

Additionally, I would like my reader(s) to be aware that this work was not intended to be read like an average novel. Each article contained herein is standalone, and one should not rely on any other reference to comprehend them. These articles can be read in any order, at any time, provided the reader understands that each piece was crafted for a specific purpose and a particular circumstance where the reader might need its definition clarified. For instance, if one seeks knowledge regarding Faith and Death, both articles can be read together without confusing the meaning behind either topic; rather, they can be read out of order or aligned with their inverse complements. Simply put, 'Start anywhere you like, and read as you will, so long as you start at the beginning of the article; this way, you can glean the beneficial quality from its written composition without losing any of its meaning or intent.'

<u>Note to the reader</u>(s):

When it comes to the following concepts: metaphysics and philosophy, the descriptions below clarify each subject and educate the reader(s) about what these terms represent. These notions include partial paraphrases and slightly modified descriptions of their defining characteristics. These excerpts were drawn from an unabridged dictionary whose name I do not remember. I have also included a direct quotation from the same reference book. This was added for continuity and to help highlight and clarify the unique phraseology used throughout this book.

The term 'Metaphysics' derives its name from several sources that, in turn, shape its definition and scope within philosophy. When philosophy is applied to any particular region of knowledge, it indicates the general laws or principles by which the contributory phenomena or facts relating to that subject can be mentally grasped. The term 'Theology' originates from the question of where the supreme power, or the divine itself, is located. Such an understanding is not only based on the superior essence that defines Life for human beings, but also on what humanity believes created its resolute and definitive nature.

Additionally, when philosophy is applied to tangible, worldly objects, the term is 'Physics.' However, when applied to human beings, the term is often associated with 'Anthropology and Psychology,' where logic and ethics are generally connected and used for consumption and understanding. However, it is called 'Philosophy' when it pertains to a specific theory or philosophical system that explains particular occurrences or events. Using this exact terminology, one can glean the feasible definitions of Reasoning, practical wisdom, argumentation, calmness of temper and judgment, serenity, fortitude, stoicism, and the nexus where misfortune intersects with philosophy.

All of philosophy's applicable characteristics are the literal terms that weave together the concepts of Love, the practical application of the search for enlightenment, and the perception, examination, and definition of any particular wonder. This concept determines the cause and reason of any random or qualified engagement, meaning those governed by the power and laws of a specific ideological belief system.

The first definition of a philosopher is one who philosophizes and is versed in or devoted to philosophy. The second is representative of one who reduces the principles of philosophy to practice in the conduct of Life, one who lives according to the rules of practical wisdom, and one who meets or regards all vicissitudes with calmness. However, to philosophize is to reason like a philosopher, to search into the reason and nature of things, and to investigate phenomena, all of which are measures meant to assign rational causes to their existence.

The following is a direct quote from Sir Walter Hamilton:

"Philosophy has been defined as the conscience of things divine and human, and the causes in which they are contained,—the science of effects by their causes,—the science of sufficient reason,—the science of things possible,—the science of things deduced from the first principles,—the science of truths sensible and abstract,—the application of reason to its legitimate objects,—the science of the relations of all knowledge to the necessary ends of human reason,—the science of the original form of the ego, or mental self,—the science of science,—the science of the absolute,—the science of the absolute indifference of the ideal and real."

In conclusion, I thoroughly enjoyed writing this extensive digest and sharing my thoughts with every reader. I anticipate that those who take the Time to peruse this exposition will be pleasantly delighted with the helpful collection of articles contained herein and find a degree of use within its humble pages to enhance their lives. I am confident that most readers will enjoy their journey through my mind, not only for the information to draw from but also for how I chose to adorn the many colorful warrens with unique and inspiring diction along the way.

...This creation is my gift to the world, and nothing would give me greater joy than to know that "My voice mattered to someone, I left a legacy behind, and I created something out of a nothing Life."

A true pleasure to share, T.C. Monk

"Here comes the orator with his flood of words and his drop of reason."

(Benjamin Franklin)

– ETERNITY –

(1)

The word "Eternity" is a noun. It is defined as existing or being in a state of existence, indefinitely, never-ending, an everlasting condition with no boundary to confine it.

* * *

At the outset of this article, I must admit that I initially had a rudimentary understanding of Eternity and found myself struggling with its structural veracity and complexity, which is not surprising given the subject matter. For clarity, the only comparison I can offer is a labyrinth with no end and an incomprehensible design. This subject required a good measure of Time and reflective meditation before I finally concluded; I could refine the concept more existentially, allowing my audience to choose how they wish to perceive it. Once this thought germinated, I understood what I decided to incorporate in this article and why.

When one wishes to tackle the subject of Eternity, one would first need to acquire a basic understanding of its intrinsic nature rather than rely on the proposed scientific theory humanity has attached to it. Engaging in such an action without an intellectual standard to define its scope would be a faux pas, entirely obscuring the clarity they seek: comprehension. Furthermore, it would be beneficial for the reader of this work to set aside any preconceived notions they may have about this subject before reading it, as this rendering is intended to offer an alternative viewpoint for considering the ambiguity of such a motif. In doing so, one might harvest more from examining this creative production than one may realize and subsequently come away with a more limpid understanding of what it means to comprehend its quiddity.

It is essential to emphasize that Eternity is not a simple concept to describe or define, as its essence evokes profound humility. Several of the fundamental themes I will discuss in this article align with the general school of thought most people adopt, which is taught from a young age. Some of the information presented will be drawn from academic sources, including descriptive language and definitions. However, the remainder will reflect the knowledge and understanding I have acquired regarding its existence and uniformity.

Consider this: when humans think of the word Eternity, their initial thoughts are bound to one of the following categories (if not all):

1) The unfathomable expanse of the universe.
2) What encompasses everything.
3) A sense of Time, and
4) An immeasurable distance.

The things that fall within the realm humans define as Eternity are mere shades of these four governing notions. But why does humanity think in such a restrictive manner? Why only four columns? Does this not contradict the fundamental concept of endlessness? One could pose the latter query, but the honest answer is that there must be a limit to everything in creation, including the parameters of the infinite and their application to both thought and design.

THE TIES THAT BIND

Strangely, humans often use the term 'limitless' when defining things. Such an endeavor smacks of uncertainty and a desperate need for closure, yet this is how the mind works. It boils down to the need for an index, a framework to codify items for Future recognition. Even if the details are somewhat tentative, this at least provides a baseline for what it is attempting to classify. There will be Time later to address any corrective measures for such hypotheses, especially if an error is discovered in their structural design.

I do not intend to be accusatory, mordant, or overly detailed in my recitation, but such is necessary to expose the truth within the body of my descriptive narration. Most humans tend to compare themselves to what they read, as it draws on a desire to know whether they act or think the same way it is written. And, even though this is a faulty and unreliable method of self-examination, there is nothing deleterious with this form of comparative association, as long as one recognizes the importance of retractive and reformative thinking. Such is not a natural proclivity or measure of actuation employed by every human mind, but rather a requirement to be mindful of, especially if they wish to avoid public ridicule for cutting corners or a lack of professional due diligence.

With that being said, shall we proceed down the rabbit hole? Good, then "follow meeeee..."

$$\mathbb{T} \cap \mathbb{T}$$

Most humans understand that Eternity encompasses all things in existence (See category #2 of this section) and that all necessary elements in equal and opposing measures exist within its folds.

These allotments exist in the required combination and degree. No force, in and of itself, is more crucial than any other. Their apportionment is precisely formulated to maintain the equilibrium of creation throughout Life's cosmic tapestry.

The mental perception of existence that most people devise for themselves is not only a method of organized assimilation but also a means of identifying the structure of all things they have come to know. Humans must create such a framework, as it establishes a focal point—the true center of balance — between the terminal points of Life's spectrum. The crafting of these prodigious thoughts by humanity not only aligns with humankind's curious nature but also feeds its ego and its assumed superiority.

Furthermore, it fosters a measure of gradation that establishes a causal connection between all things in one's perceived reality. And, even though the defining boundary and nature of its essence are verily unknown to humanity, its unwavering presence remains a prominent and controlling factor in its ever-changing macrocosm. It is quite a mystery why one cannot marvel at being aware of such a unique aspect. Every day, I am in awe of its wondrous existence. I have always thought, "The treasures of Eternity carry a temporal value, all of which are woven by the graceful hands of Time and meted by the subtle touch of Death." – T.C. Monk

Eternity measures the balance of deficiency with necessity, progress with conformity, and creation with detraction. All of these factors are prerequisites for the building blocks of Life design, and each has its own designated parts for specific purposes. Nothing in the physical universe comes or is enacted without an assigned plan of action attached. There is no set method of construction woven around it, nor is it devised without its coequal dependents as part of its design structure, other than its nature being telescopic.

However, there is much to contemplate regarding Eternity, but where does one begin? The concept of Eternity is thought to have no beginning, no end, and no definitive composition one can perceive beyond the assumed. How does one even attempt to contemplate the abstruse probabilities of such a notion? The possibility of this is doubtful, as humanity's current knowledge is genuinely inadequate to comprehend the scope of its penultimate form.

I'd like to share a brief story for all my readers to consider. This is relevant to the article's overall theme and also showcases another aspect of my writing prowess, which may enhance the impression I make.

– I had a dream about Eternity a Time ago, which left a keen impression on my mind and generated the impulse and desire to script this entire compilation. Its overall sense was not something I would be comfortable imparting or convincing anyone of being divinely inspired, as I do not ascribe to such assumptions; instead, I tagged it as a manifestation of the undisciplined mind. And, based upon this extrapolation, I am not only convinced that it is the veritable nature by which the mind conscripts the amorphous reality of the unknown, but also how it contrives anything it needs at the moment, even proffering itself a clear-cut definition of a thing it previously lacked any knowledge regarding. How such is possible, I could not explain.

Usually, when I awaken from a dream, I cannot recall most - if any - of the details, but in this particular instance, my mind seemed to latch onto the contrived eidos like a steel trap. Within the chimera, my consciousness felt completely absent. The only perceivable thing in my field of vision was an immense structure, a reasonable distance from my current locus. Although I could see it, I could not determine its true nature because my vision was limited by its immense size. I could feel how real it was, yet its presence was indefinable, and my mind was at a loss for comprehension. Its substance appeared solid, but its essence undulated slowly within an invisible barrier, much as the contents of a gaseous planet are contained within its scope of regulatory control —the corollary of gravity.

Its presence was neither menacing nor threatening. Still, the proximity of its existence to my general being gave off the impression that it was deceptively massive. Yet, somehow, ultimately constrained like a sponge stuffed into an undersized container it was never meant to occupy, straining to break free. Even though I was on the exterior of this globe-like mass, I somehow understood with absolute certainty what was inside its boundary. It was the universe I came from, the one I was born within. I realized I was outside my realm of existence, but could not fathom how to discern this impression amid my nescience. Although it just felt like a self-evident truth, something indisputable, a stubborn fact.

The moment I captured the uncultivated comprehension of what I was viewing, it bred a sinister Fear in me like nothing else I had ever felt before. Its embodiment was so absolute, so piercing, and beyond refutation, I began to shake uncontrollably. I was terrified beyond description. Past familiarity, and with every fiber of my being, I sought reentry - pleaded silently for it - as I felt the unequivocal and painful quiddity of being alone, abandoned, cast out among the nothingness, consigned to oblivion. At that moment, I understood the cold, keen, and arrant nature of existing in the desolation beyond the verge of creation's province, outside Time's scope of existence.

In that same temporal span, a sudden phrase flashed across my mind, one I did not recognize the meaning of, which kind of irked me, as I took pride in my mental discernment and knowledge of language, which seemed a bit shallow to consider at that moment. The phrase reads, 'Everything Time Eventually Renders Nature Intended To, Yot.' I was actually at a loss for its latter meaning. It wasn't until much later, when I wrote it down, that I realized it was an acronym for "Eternity." I then did some quick research on the word, 'Yot.' I realized it was an archaic term meaning 'To unite closely,' which brought instant clarity to its descriptive intent and summoned to mind a closely related simile by William Blake: 'Eternity is in Love with the creations of Time.' Somatology in its penultimate form, wow!

Just before I awoke, I thought about the pieces in this exhibition. I realized that if this was what it felt like to be omniscient, to possess the perspective of an omnipotent entity, I did not wish to claim ownership of such an eidos. My only desire in the dream was to return home, climb back inside the sphere, and be once again bound within the domain of my comfortable and ignorant reality. Such an overlet of recognition and understanding was never meant to be revealed or possessed by humankind. Its immense nature is incomprehensible to the limited boundaries of our minds. –

Okay, back to the main article.

Speaking of the poet William Blake, I ask the reader to meditate on this next section, particularly the first four lines Blake penned in his poem, 'Auguries of Innocence.' This will be necessary when contemplating the type of boundlessness I refer to in this article. The inclusion of this unique work here demonstrates how well Blake's concept aligns with the parameters of this creation and the conceptual framework it can offer the reader. So, please take the Time to consider the following incorporation. And yes, it is a fragment of the poem, but it holds more than one might assume.

The first four lines of Blake's poem are as follows:

'To see a world in a grain of sand,
and a heaven in a wildflower,
hold infinity in the palm of your hand,
and Eternity in an hour.'

This unique quatrain by Blake holds so much meaning and depth that one should marvel at how brilliantly he implies such a profusion of conceptual associations. However, the only disappointing aspect of his thoughtful creation is that these four lines are the only ones in the poem that differ from the rest. This entire section appears to have been written separately and not tailored for this particular production. So, let us take a gander at the first verse:

'To see a world in a grain of sand,'

Take a second or two to ponder this line. Imagine if it were possible to see a world in a grain of sand.' If so, what type of world might one see? What novel beauties might one discover? Would one spend an Eternity peeking into each new world they find? Would one even stop to consider how much sand there is in our world? Would one ever view the beach in the same way again? And, if one could see a world in each grain, would they even ponder how much sand might exist on each new world they looked upon?

Furthermore, could one even contemplate how many times this concept could be exponentially multiplied? And could such a multitude even be imagined? I assume not to any particular, quantifiable degree, as such a feat of intellect is beyond any scope humans can deduce or translate into any comprehensive relation. The structure of Eternity is much more complicated than one could possibly comprehend. If the current information indicates what may genuinely exist beyond humanity's capacity to understand, then such a concept is an incredibly terrifying and awe-inspiring realization.

Although it would be nice to assume one can imagine such grandiose proportions, trying to grasp such a measure would be comparable to calculating one's Life expectancy and the exact moment of its expiration. Infinite scales such as these are beyond one's capacity to discern in any actual sense.

Let us move on to the second verse:

'And a heaven in a wild flower,'

Consider the possibility that such a vision in Life could be perceived. Would the availability of such a visual reference diminish or detract from its quaint beauty? If it were possible to see 'a heaven in a wildflower,' would one be capable of fathoming how many wildflowers might exist in this world? Would one even take a moment to consider how many wildflowers might exist within each heaven they look upon, or the myriad types of new genera they may discover?

Furthermore, how many heavens might exist if there were a heaven within every wildflower? Is it possible to conceive the magnitude each notion intimates or its volume? Such a concept is an enormous reality for the mind to consider. Whatever answers these contemplative motifs may generate, they are food for thought and matters beyond one's ability to perceive accurately in any knowledgeable fashion.

Now, to the third line of this quatrain:

'Hold infinity in the palm of your hand,'

Could one even picture or comprehend holding the nature of infinity in the palm of one's hand? If this concept were remotely possible, imagine what one might be capable of having in the palm of one's other hand. The implications of such an idea are immeasurable within the human mind. Is one even capable of speculating on some level about the impression of such? If so, does this connote a perceivable boundary, a limitation to its influence, structural uncertainty, and obscure meaning? But then again, does not some measure of infinity rest in the palm of one's hand at any given moment? One would assume as much, but pondering such queries is quite a problem.

Finally, let us examine the last verse in this specific production:

'And Eternity in an hour.'

This concept is abstruse at best and is undoubtedly paradoxical. To know 'Eternity in an hour' is an impossible thought even to consider, as Eternity itself implies the absence of limitation upon the gamut of its existence. However, for argument's sake, let us take a moment to reflect upon the question it poses.

If one could know 'Eternity in an hour,' how many hours could exist in the Eternity of Time? Could such a measure gauge Eternity? Would this idea by Blake be suggestive of an endless existence in Eternity? Or does this position propose a line of demarcation within Eternity itself? Either point holds merit and presents alternate possibilities, but I would posit that nothing is beyond consideration when it comes to Eternity.

Here is where I would question whether these theories are subjects fit for consideration or matters one should contemplate the depths of, given the diametrically opposite suppositions. I would assume not; then again, why not? Allow me to take a moment to propose and examine (for the reader) the counterpoints of Eternity in the fashion humanity comprehends it.

If Blake were being literal when he crafted the third and fourth segments of the poem I referenced, this would imply that such concepts are limited in scope. His rendering would not allow one to consider the idea of true illimitability. And, if this is how he intended it to be perceived, then how could either prospect be what humans term them to be? They could not! However, what if Blake was being less literal and more symbolic when he scripted those lines? Maybe his idea was to give the impression that 'What the mind can imagine, so too can it believe.'

Keeping with this theme, is it feasible to humanity that Blake's idea of infinity and Eternity was more geared toward one's ability to notice the veneer of one's own Life and how it is in stark contrast to the profundity of creation? If so, then Blake's ultimate intent was to utilize terrestrial measures to show one could hold the concept of: * 'A secret world among the unknown, a touch of perfection in an untamed universe, infinity as a bound prodigy, and the limit of

Eternity in the mind's eye.' *(A line-for-line comparison with those of Blake's poem.)

Furthermore, if one could hold such notions in the mind's eye, it might be possible to realize just how limitless its gifts truly are and how humans are part of its infinite configuration. This quaint revelation (through his eyes) conveys that the most incredible gift humans possess is the boundless breadth of their imagination.

This is my interpretation of the first four lines of his poem, read figuratively or metaphorically. I do not claim this to be his true intent, but rather an abstract notion of what he may have been trying to convey. It was a joy to read most of Blake's work and a humble Honor to be fortunate enough to touch on it in my lifetime and Present my thoughts alongside his creation.

Defining Eternity as it truly is would be impossible for anyone, unless it were not for the definition humanity has assumed. People may think they know or form beliefs through inductive and deductive reasoning, but this supposition does not accurately capture their essence. Even if one could situate Eternity within a framework conforming to human specifications, it would defeat the purpose of quantifying it. An action such as this would significantly limit the scope of exploration for those inclined to hypothesize the nature of its orphic composition.

Humanity's capacity to understand such a notion is limited by the quality of experience gained in Life and the equitable knowledge one can affix to its complement. Such are the compatible measures employed to interpret the Eternity theorem, as humanity has defined this concept for themselves, its boundary, and what is ascribed to its nature.

If one truly wishes to contemplate this notion, the real question here should be, "Why do humans exist in creation?" Or,

"Are we special?" But such questions raise others: "Should one query such things?" If so, why? If not, why not? Would one assume their existence is in some way eternal? Does this imply the possibility that one may be born again within creation's tapestry? If so, will they somehow be elevated to another plane of existence? If not, will they be replaced by another of Eternity's superior creations?

Hmm, quite the enigma to ponder, as no one truly knows the answers to such museful concepts. Most people can hypothesize, theorize, and debate such propositional issues at their leisure. Still, such thoughts will remain in flux and most likely confound humanity for Eternity.

With that being said, should humans accept Eternity as it is, understand it has always been (as far as we know), and not bother to question or reflect upon its nature? This author would strenuously object to the latter being any acceptable verity, primarily since humans exist in a reality where all living things perish. Everything in existence should be questioned, pondered, and reflected upon. Its very constitution demands such inquiry into its obscure formation. Such a measure is geared toward extracting a logical understanding of its unique and cryptic nature, as well as the extent to which humanity directly influences its embodiment.

Furthermore, in considering one's relevance and the extent to which one can impact existence in a meaningful sense, this author believes that human Life is too short even to make a difference in Eternity. Our species is too insignificant in the grand scheme of things to really matter. It is doubtful that even if humans were gifted a million lifetimes, they would still be incapable of making any considerable mark upon its canvas. This reminds me of a short passage I penned in my second book, entitled *Daedal Convergence,* which reads:

> 'In comparison to Eternity, I am
> but a flash in Time, like stray embers
> rising from a fire pit ... gone in
> an instant and easily forgotten.'

In summary, I am confident that the abstract impression of Eternity humans have created for themselves is merely a sense of their place within the infinite, and it is this essence that will, and does, dominate all that has been and will ever be.

– TIME –

(2)

The word "Time" is a noun. It is defined as the infinite and continued progress of existence or events in the Past, Present, and Future regarded as a whole. Time also refers to a calculated interval between two points in Time.

* * *

When contemplating the structure of this article and how to Present it, I was genuinely confused about where to begin this version. It could not be at the beginning, as I was not there and did not know its origin. I couldn't start at the end, as this has yet to come, and trying to start in the middle only confused me further. I thought about it for a spell, then decided to attack it from multiple angles, utilizing what I knew of its presence in my Life while postulating what lay beyond.

Time is a simple word. It consists of only four letters and has a straightforward description. But it would be incorrect to assume such a thought, as Time has confounded and haunted humankind for millennia. There are thousands of thoughts, ideas, and questions about Time. Most humans have formed their own opinions about this notion, yet they have no genuine desire to contemplate its profundity beyond what they already know or what has been outlined for them. This undertaking will allow the reader to dispel any preconceived notions of Time, leaving themselves open to suggestive contemplation. After that, one can gain a more lucid understanding of the concept humans have created for their own purposes.

The essence of Time is a uniquely complex phenomenon and a notion that is difficult to define accurately. So, for clarity, I will posit that Time is not a stationary concept, nor is it inextricably bound to a particular parameter by which it can be measured, as it has no actual construct, substance, or meaning other than what humans have attached to it. Maybe Einstein was correct when he said, "Time is a stubbornly persistent illusion." – (*Collateral Damage*, 2016)

The notion of Time humans have constructed needs further clarification, while leaving its boundaries open to expansion and personal interpretation. Although my intent for scripting this article has several different points of reference I wish to elaborate upon, particularly those that evoke a multitude of questions others may not have thought to consider before perusing the contents of this creation:

1) Is to shed some light upon the concept of its creation by humanity.

2) Is to question the purpose of its existence in our reality.

3) To bring a deeper understanding of its ambiguous nature to others.

4) To question its authenticity, design structure, and functionality.

5) It is not to pigeonhole Time, as it is not bound to a linear frame of reference, other than from inception to termination as humans know it.

These points of concern are meant to provide not only a broader sense of the nature humanity has devised and attached to it, but also a stark contrast to the simple, come-and-go prospect it is known to embody. To address it in any other fashion would reflect what has already been dissected myriad Times, which is something other than what I wish to employ.

The substance of Time is not a physical manifestation one can discern with the senses, like that of a star, the wind, or any other object one can experience in Life. It is more of an embodiment humans have manufactured out of necessity, serving as a baseline for defining what is known. This concept is based on a pattern of perceived movement and is characterized by sentient awareness, its degree of interaction, spatial displacement, and its range of retraction. The relative perception of Time is tentative in nature and governed by calculable movement. It has its foundations in the physical reality in which humans dwell and in that which gives Time its recognizable structure.

In this author's opinion, Time is the architect of all creation, but not the sole creator. Despite being a contrived concept fashioned by humanity, the sheer breadth of its scope and the timbre of its pulse offer the illusion that it is real. But how can this be if Time does not exist outside the R.I.N.G. humanity has woven around it? This R.I.N.G. refers to the creation of Time's restrictive scope of measurability and to why it is bound to a circular, repetitive range of accountability familiar to all humans, as represented by a clock. (R.I.N.G.- Rotating In Natural Graduation.)

*Humanity's modern conception of Time is relatively new. It is often thought to have been created or invented, much like any other object in the known world, but this needs to be corrected. It would be more accurate to say that humans first became aware of Time by observing the movement of the heavenly bodies during the prehistoric era, approximately 30,000 years ago.

During antiquity, the Babylonians were thought to have been the first to develop a system of mathematical computation based on the number 60 and the 360-day year, which is believed to have occurred around 1600 B.C.E. Although, about a hundred years later, as early as 1500 B.C.E., the Egyptians were known to have created Sundials to establish a qualitative standard of tracking Time based on the Sun's movement, which was common back then during the seasonal Times for consistency in agriculture. *(Wikipedia, 2019) *

I remember the first Time I learned about the Sundial. It was in grade school, during a history lesson regarding advanced civilizations. The teacher (Ms. Michigan) ushered our class outside to the playground. She waited until all the students had queued up by the sandbox before instructing each of us to create rudimentary Sundials on the surface of the sand, then place a stick upright at their center and submerge a portion of it beneath the surface. As we were acting out this scenario, she began to explain the concept of using directional orientation to find North and to estimate the relative Time of day from her watch. This is where I first became aware that the Sun still casts a shadow at high noon, depending on one's locus on the planet. It is not a perfect science, but rather a comparative form from which to extract a workable model.

THE TIES THAT BIND

Time's current state is approximately three to four centuries into its creation stage. This estimate would roughly correspond to the Time when humans attempted to establish a more precise and consistent framework for measuring it. This was to institute an ecumenical standard worldwide based upon Galileo's invention of the pendulum in the 17th Century. However, no one can honestly say with certainty how long Time existed for human beings, or how many people attempted to structure it for the masses before Galileo. One can surmise such, but this would defeat the purpose of knowing.

Every essence in the known universe can be measured with Time in one fashion or another. The Life expectancy of all things is vital to temporal beings (humans), as they are familiar with its restrictive mode of existence and hold a relative kinship to that which is finite. A relation like this is meant to foster conscious connection among all things.

In the previous article, 'Eternity,' reference was made to the 'Eternity of Time.' The allusion was intended to reveal a connection between the two, thereby highlighting its existence. And even though most humans would adamantly object to Time and Eternity appearing together in the same context (assuming one is finite, the other infinite), they are both latent in one another, based on humanity's understanding of them, and not diametrically opposed as one might assume. For either of these concepts to even be linked together in theory, the foundation of each must be latent in the other's creation.

Consider this: Without Time, one could not mentally discern any sense of Eternity's breadth, and without Eternity, one could not verily assess Time as a quantifiable source of valuation or mean distance of measure. One can see this in the definition of a light year and in how it is computed.

The distance of such a standard could not be calculated without Time as a coequal integer of its equation, hence Einstein's formula for $E=mc^2$. This mathematical expression references:

E (energy)
= (equals)
m (mass)
[Times]
c (constant) [the speed of light]
^{2} (squared)

Time's equation rests in this pattern of expression. How can this scientific notion be calculated without knowing the Time it takes light to travel? It is postulated that light travels at 186,000 miles per second (MPS), which is approximately 6 trillion miles per year, highlighting the crucial role of Time in this calculation.

When humans think of trillions of miles, the immediate thought is, 'How long will it take to span that distance?', hence the need for the alternate equation in this formula, which begs the question of, "How long will it take a human to travel one light year, rather at our current best rate of speed, or at the speed of light?" These are two particular methods of movement (speed and Time), which must be calculated together for one to formulate and comprehend the conclusion sought.

Eternity implies an incalculable distance. However, humans have measured it using Time as the universal standard. This actuation represents a specific degree or extent of travel rather than pure thought or actual physical movement. It may not be a straightforward rule for every particular thing in existence. Still, it is when one attempts to measure any distance humans wish to travel. The operative term to remember when considering the above content is - 'distance.' This notion of Time is calibrated, woven into every sense of the word, and not a factor that can be reckoned without it. If not, then why calibrate, gauge, or measure a distance to begin with, if not for the desire to know how long it will take to get there? Distance is undoubtedly a measure of Time's breath within Eternity if one genuinely considers it.

I have spent a great deal of Time examining this concept and trying to understand all the angles of its development and application. For anyone to suggest that Time and Eternity are not coequal forces is something one should ponder a little longer and consider more thoroughly before assuming any definitive position. Anyone taking a stance such as this without proper examination and evaluation would expose themselves to misinformation.

In the general parameters of Life, most humans speak of Time in the same sense that it has no limit, no boundaries, and nothing can escape its touch nor outrun it. The reality of Time is quite tricky to define in any other way than the way humans need to interpret it for themselves. It is odd to even think of Time as having a substance that can be calculated or gauged in such a way, particularly now that Time has assumed the role of measuring human Life expectancy and does not actually exist as a tangible device one can modify, disarm, destroy, or reset its design parameters.

It is rather strange to consider the myriad ways humans have measured the duration of Time. There are Periods, schedules, seasons, moments, dimensions, and evolutions of Time. These are just a few parcels of its measure, not the only ones that exist. One should be capable of grasping the number of definitions implied rather than having them listed herein.

However, why did humans feel the need to define such a thing in the first place? Was it to find out if it really exists? And, if it does, is it because humans need to understand its abstract function in the universe? Was it a concept humanity created to calculate the mean distance of their lives? Or, was it something instituted to give humans a sense of passing, of things that once were? Does anyone really know? Probably not, but the one certainty in all this is that there is nothing else in the world more important to humanity, nothing in existence that humans have dedicated themselves to measuring with such precision as that of Time.

Consider the following list of questions carefully, then attempt to answer them for yourself:

1) Is Time prejudiced?

2) Does Time only target the living?

3) Was Time in existence before all things?

4) Does anything exist outside of Time?

5) Is Time itself the creator?

6) Is Time beyond one's ability to comprehend/ understand its true nature?

7) Does this essence humans allude to, their particular method of interpreting what has been dubbed Time?

8) Is it possible to know the answers to any of these? Some could argue several issues here for amusement, but the actual answers will remain a constant mystery.

Earlier in this article, an allusion to Time was made in the phrase 'From inception to termination.' This citation is intended to reveal a span of Time that only refers to the known cycles of Life and Death as it applies to all biological Life. It was not meant to establish Time as a bounded concept or to manipulate it into any state other than the one it was intended to reflect. This last statement coincides with a maxim I wrote in 2002, which reads: "The sands of Time allow one to perceive the progressive threads of Life, the essence of its wholeness in motion, and the results of its physical reaction upon everything in its scope of regulatory sway." – T.C. Monk

Humanity observes Time as a linear form of existence for all mortal Life constructs. This perception method was established to clock its mortality, as Time does not conform to any accurate design parameters. Suppose one takes a moment to notice Life around them. In that case, they will see Time exists and radiates in all directions simultaneously, much like an expanding bubble emanating from the hypocenter of an explosion. It does not follow any particular course or pre-measured guideline, at least not on any level humans can comprehend or perceive beyond what is already presumed.

Yes, Time is expanding at all points, yet it never seems to contract... or does it? One can only see its effects when Death comes for them. Is this really a contraction, though? Or is it simply a completion of another cycle of Time? There is no way to know which concept is viable with certainty. However, the more acceptable and logical form would be the latter. Humanity should be grateful that it has learned to arrange Time in a way that allows it to perceive its transitory nature. It is not likely that the concept of Life would hold the same prodigious attraction it does now if they had not.

Now, what would an article about Time be without touching on the aspect every human being has fantasized about and wished they could engage in at some point in their Life? Can you, the reader, surmise what this may be? It is Time travel. Just the thought of this subject allows one to dream of a different Life, an alternate Time, and the ability to change anything they desire. Others might snub their noses at such a ridiculous notion, but everyone is entitled to ponder whatever they wish and even discount those they cannot fathom or realistically process.

Regarding Time travel, I am guilty of subscribing to both schools of thought, dreaming, and discounting. As a teenager, I seriously hankered to travel through Time's corridor, especially after reading 'The Time Machine' by H.G. Wells. I desperately wanted to slide back in Time and visit many of the people and places I had read and heard about, such as Socrates, Confucius, Charles Martel, Queen Victoria, Bodicea, Rome, Greece, and the infamous Atlantis, at the height of their power... to name a few. I also desired to observe the Big Bang, the creation of the stars, our world, and the inception of humanity.

However, as I matured and became much wiser, I began to understand how illogical it was to consider this prospect. Someone else's opinion did not taint my view that the notion of Time travel is impossible; it was based on my reasoning and understanding of truth. Sure, I read several books on the subject, even a few scholarly ones (the names of which escape me). Still, even those did not define my overall opinion concerning the method of travel in question. This decisive stance arose from recognizing that, for the idea of Time travel to be possible, one would need something to mark its measure, bind its location, and create a new line of deviation splitting off from its original stream.

You may ask, "What does this consist of?" Well, allow me to elucidate. There is a significant factor to consider when it comes to Time travel: a means of pegging one's actual location in a moment of Time. It would require one to possess some apparatus or mechanism that could veritably register one's physical position of existence. Without such a device, there would be no concrete evidence that one had been there, no tangible footprint of one's presence in that place or Time. But still, you may query, "What bearing would this have on Time travel?"

To articulate this more precisely, I will utilize a video camera, which is familiar to most, if not all, humans. When operational, this device can record an actual occurrence as it transpires, capturing one's location in Time. One could then rewind and replay its contents, those happenings, precisely as they unfolded, somewhat liken to human memory, but without the faulty recall. With such a device, one can capture Time as it passes, creating a tether point of origin. This establishes a stationary anchor, a physical location one can identify and target, much like a global positioning system. This is how the concept of traveling through Time becomes more plausible and more structurally sound.

Without a fixed position to record, how can one locate a specific area they intend to travel to? Without a place of origin to begin or return to, one cannot legitimately travel in Time anywhere. And, not having been Present at a specific point in Time, one could not visit such a place, as it would not exist for them or anyone else. This concept is easy to deduce from the camera details above. What I mean is that if this device records something, the only existing, viewable item will be what it captures; nothing existed before it began recording.

Consider this: say one created a Time machine and built it in their closet. Once it is functional, its actual existence begins at that moment in Time for its creator and the device. Neither oneself nor the machine will ever be able to go farther back than the moment it came into existence, nor will it be capable of traveling to any place it has not been Present. It would be relegated to the specific area where it was created and from whence it departed. The only way to change its travel point and destination would be to physically move it to a new location, much like the H.G. Wells character was forced to do in the end. The same would be true for all points, places, and periods of (or in) Time.

This should clear up any confusion about whether a device is necessary for Time travel. Whether it's a camera, one's memory, or some creation or another, it doesn't matter. The fact that a point in Time needs to be established (recorded) for it to exist as a location for one to travel to or from will be an essential factor in any conversation involving Time travel. Using a camera in this scenario was meant to showcase my point, nothing more. The mind is the perfect recording device, despite its imperfections, as it anchors us to each moment in our lives and is the only current means of Time travel.

By and through the measures in this particular piece, it is not only how humans are capable of assuming the product of their own acceptance of reality, but also how it applies to the world they so desperately wish to become a more productive element of, along with the allotments of Time and Life it readily offers to every sentient being.

– LIFE –

(3)

The word "Life" is a noun. It is defined as a period during which Life lasts, such as the span between birth and Death. It is also the fragile duration during which things exist and can function within such parameters.

* * *

When I began to tackle this inspiring theme, I aimed to script it in a way that would take the reader on a journey of sentient existence, allowing them to come away with a unique perspective on how its concept can be perceived more expansively than they already comprehend. I have no desire to impose a personal agenda on anyone; rather, I want to offer them a perspective on what Life has taught me. Using this method of engagement, I aim to define it in a way that enables others to use my opinion, alongside their own, to contemplate what the truth is for themselves, whether their own version or a combination of both.

There is no Doubt that the notion of Life is a remarkable undertaking for anyone to explore, as "Life is not a mystery to be solved, but an experience to be endured" (Paraphrased from the Film Dune, 2021). The sheer scope of its vivid artistry tends to elicit awe in viewers, showering their vision and spirit with a wealth of emotional enchantment. The unique beauty it offers is far more dazzling and expressive in reality than what words could ever capture. It reminds me of some feedback I received about this work and a poem that supports the expression of Life I intend to convey in this article.

The author wrote about the bridge between the human and natural worlds, highlighting how they often lack the expressive language and consciousness to communicate their unique interconnectedness. – (Courtesy of 'The Pen Project,' Spring class of 2021 – Intern, Almalena) The following is the poem she shared with me.

"Breakage" by <u>Mary</u> <u>Oliver</u>
I go down to the edge of the sea.
How everything shines in the morning light!
The cusp of the whelk,
the broken cupboard of the calm,
the opened, blue mussels,
moon snails, pale pink and barnacle scarred—
and nothing at all whole or shut, but tattered, split,
dropped by the gulls onto gray rocks, and all the moisture gone.
It's like a schoolhouse
of little words,
thousands of words.
First, you figure out what each one means by itself,
the jingle, the periwinkle, the scallop,
full of moonlight.

Then you begin, slowly, to read the whole story.

Given the communicative phrasing in the above paragraph, despite any expressive measures one might utilize to describe or define the ineffable nature of Life, it would only be possible for some to truly relate to its essence. Any other attempt would surely fall short of such an endeavor. However, when attempting to survey Life in Kind, its eidos may allow one to contemplate such matters on a scale far different from that typically employed. It will allow for hypothesis and postulation beyond expanding one's range of perceptibility and the extent of appreciation and poignant delineation. The humble feelings its essence can evoke might cause one to become intoxicated by its spell and enraptured by the magnificent, creative display rendered before their eyes.

There is no question that the ever-changing kaleidoscope of Life is one of incredible design and intense color. It is doubtful there is anything in existence capable of equaling its pageantry, outshining its majesty, or surpassing its ingenuity. Whatever is weaving its decorative tapestry should not be dismissed, overlooked, or underappreciated. It is too expressive to be an inanimate force. Some incorporeal substance must drive it, a thing beyond one's ability to perceive or comprehend meaningfully. In the creative sphere of Life, I have come to realize that nothing is equal; not even the power of imagination, which can conceive or dream of anything, can match its essence. It is an incredible dichotomy to be part of, as it pulls the mind in myriad directions simultaneously and requires equal temperance to balance it out. How this is possible remains unknown, thereby becoming just another part of Life's miraculous formation.

That said, I often wonder if it is possible to gain an advantage when there is no set baseline to Life's shifting configuration. Suppose humans decide to approach Life one labor at a Time. In that case, they could gain a stable and worthwhile constitution from its variety. It is this maddening uncertainty that makes Life exciting and worth the struggle. Such an engagement is rather frustrating and confusing, but beneficial for those fortunate enough to summon the will to endure its arduous journey. It reminds me of a quote that echoes this with clarity: "Don't pray for an easy Life; pray for the strength to endure a difficult one." – (Bruce Lee)

Life is complicated in structure and quite impossible to define definitively. Its complex nature makes it difficult to understand how and why it is contrived, so that one could spend an Eternity trying to puzzle out its confounding nature. There are so many aspects to its composition that it would be an obscene challenge to find a perfect angle from which to view its embodiment, as such conditions Present a unique perspective for one to ponder the point of view each new bearing offers the eye.

The sentiment in the above paragraph refers to how impossible it is to see its true glory, no matter how one casts their vision. I remember going out into the woods when I was young, back in Warren, Ohio, and marveling at the myriad displays of creation around me: The insects, flowers, weeds, dirt, grass, shrubs, animals, the diffuse light falling through the canopy of leaves above, and the soft wind soughing through the sparse sylvan around me. Back then, I didn't know how to appreciate it for what it was, but I certainly do now, and oh, how I miss it so!

However, the most overwhelming aspect for me was how to prompt my mind to capture it all. There are so many details to take in, so many things to wonder about. How could one not become enamored or lost trying to absorb it all? To this very day, I still admire its magnificence and wonder if anyone else has ever experienced the same profound sense of awe that affects them upon viewing such an ostentatious spectacle.

Now, when it comes to human beings, our species is essentially created from a paradigm that mimics itself infinitely, with only slight variations to distinguish it from other copies. The infrastructure of Life design is an extensive web of infinite proportions. Its pattern is repetitive and transpires across the entire breadth of the cosmos. It is similar to the daedal forms in nature called 'Fractals,' those which appear to be nonpareil replicas of themselves. It represents deliberate and conscious architecture, not by accident or luck. How anyone can miss the presence of such a limpid and premeditated act is quite astonishing!

Speaking of nonpareil replicas, consider the intricate design of a snowflake. Does the average person take the Time to contemplate how it's formed? Several scientific articles have attempted to explain the hypothesis by examining factors such as wind velocity, temperature, height, rate of descent, and air density. Still, definitive proof of its exact geometric pattern formation has not yet been established. Such positions are merely illations shared by the scientific community, nothing more.

Consider its formation (the snowflake). Compare this to how an ice cube forms. My reference in this resides in the need for a formative instrument, a template to create them, a product of theorem (provable science), a result that can be perceived and comprehended visually and applied practically. A snowflake does not utilize a form of organization as humans know it. However, it is still uniform in its geometric construction - all of them - causing one to wonder how this is possible in such a manner.

However, what if one does not limit their perception to the human species alone but expands it to encompass the entire mosaic of creation? If they did, then one might find more of the same models reproducing on a massive scale, such as Animals after their kind, plants, stars, planets, single-celled organisms, microbes, and a flurch of other primal matter (energy-driven substances) in our physical universe. To consider the magnitude of this system's complexity and vastness, one would be immediately overwhelmed by the sheer profusion of visible elements bombarding them, as well as the invisible ones that unknowingly affect their surroundings.

It is strange to think of Life as a continuous representation of cause and effect. Still, its cogent factor is a reality, something likened to a palindrome - forward and backward - and reflects what Henri Bergson said, "What is found in effect, was already in the cause." So, if the causalities are related (latent in one another), can one not assume their natural graduation is autogenous and self-perpetuating? It makes perfect sense since both concepts are germane in form and function. The symmetry of this framework offers a unique perspective on how the synthesis of this continuum responds to the process and effects of synergy.

Nothing about Life is simple. It must be broken down into its constituent parts to fully understand its auspicious nature. Such an act is necessary to itemize and categorize human behavior and perception. This factor is essential to engaging humanity's Life cycles for Future recognition and proper utilization.

Consider this: in antiquity, Plato taught something akin to perfection in creation. His concept referred to the existence of a Platonic form in nature that, whether one is referring to an animal or some other item, the reality is that there exists a model that is independent of what one's mind has contrived for them, and that there exists a more perfect form of any particular item than what one is actually seeing.

Without such notions to contemplate or teachings to draw from, one would be prone to making the same type of mistakes perpetually due to the inherent nature of trial and error. By using such methods of evaluation and mean representation, one can learn from each engagement and thereby become progressive without

sentiment with clarity: "If you do not go after what you want, you'll be forced to accept what you are given." – (Nora Roberts)

In summary, if one takes a moment to gaze upon the fabric of Life and its myriad facets, one may recognize that it is reminiscent of an elaborate dome of kaleidoscopic glass that separates the fragments into a masterpiece of color without flaw. Its essence will continue to subtly shade its mosaic from every angle, even as Death slowly grinds its pulchritude into dust.

– DEATH –

(4)

The word "Death" is a noun. It is defined as the terminal, irreversible end of Life and the destruction or permanent cessation of any living thing.

* * *

As I approached the outline for this topic, I was intimidated by what the concept evoked and how much I would need to flesh out its embodiment. After further contemplation, I concluded there was no need to overly accentuate the details of its presentation. The amount of festooning I initially considered, for clarity and consumption, would be unnecessary and likely need clarification to maintain the overall message, dulling its shine.

Initially, I was uncertain about where to start this piece, as the subject has many facets to its production. Still, it soon became apparent that I should start with how I first came to experience Death in my Life and how it affected me. This thought led me to include the following story herein. I want to apologize in advance if this content is too graphic for some readers. Still, I felt it necessary to Present it in this manner to emphasize its relative importance, how it shaped the Future of my development, and how this particular event also helped me understand the nature of its significance. (Certain names have been changed to protect their identities.)

That said, I will begin with the unfortunate incident that occurred while I was visiting my friend Donnie at his parents' house. I was twelve years old at the Time. I resided at the Arizona Children's Home in Tucson, Arizona, a place I had been ordered to attend by the juvenile court system for my less-than-appropriate actions as an adolescent.

- The Reynold's house was a modest structure of red adobe brick, lined with a darker mortar. It sported white shutters, a matching picket fence, and silver-and-bronze wind chimes crowning its front porch. A metallic blue and gold Chevy Malibu, with whitewall tires and chrome moon rims, was parked beneath its oil-stained carport. The landscape of the foreyard was covered with a plethora of variegated gravel, neatly necklacing both sides of the mandarin-colored flagstones of the front walkway.

At this visit to my friend's house, I sat at the serving counter (facing into the kitchen), eating lunch and trading playful slights with my buddy Donnie. His dad (Brett) was in the kitchen cleaning up lunch service. His mom was at work, and his eleven-year-old sister, Danni Lynn, sat at the dining table behind us, having just come from the hallway.

Donnie and I giggled like hapless idiots, talking about girls and Star Wars action figures, when a sudden loud crack split the air inside the house like a thunderclap. The loud issuance instantly startled me. At the exact moment I heard and felt the concussive shock wave, my hands immediately covered my ears, and I abruptly fell off the tall stool I had been seated on in fright. I swiftly attempted to locate the origin of the sound as I hit the floor, understanding its issuance had come from the rear of where I had been seated moments ago.

When I finally located the source, the scene that proffered itself held me in thrall for several long seconds before my paralysis kicked in and allowed me to move. I quickly felt the nausea of Fear begin to rise in my throat, and my skin blistered with horripilation (goosebumps). My nose stung, and my eyes teared up as I absorbed and processed the macabre scene. The only way I could describe the feeling at the Time was to say my whole body was suffering from a severe state of antipathy, an unwillingness to believe or accept the realistic realism of reality.

There, at the dining room table opposite the kitchen, sitting in a chair against the back wall, was Donnie's little sister, Danni Lynn. As I looked upon her, I noticed that a portion of the left side of her head was missing, open to the air, and there was a thick mottling of blood and gray matter covering the wall behind her. A black and dun-colored shotgun (sawed-off) lay on the floor beneath the table, barrel smoking like a thick cigar.

I scrambled to my feet, eyes clocking the front door, eager for escape. However, I did not move toward it, as my focus had shifted to Donnie's dad, Brett. He had instantly appeared at Danni Lynn's side, calling out to her, his voice filled with dismay. What he did next completely baffled me. Confusion and revulsion struck me like a church bell shattering the night's silence.

I noticed Brett's frame shake as he began scooping up bits of gray matter from the table with one hand while gently pulling strands of Danni Lynn's bloodstained blond hair from the wall with the other. He tried desperately and tenderly to place these items back onto and into her half-open skull, all the while speaking softly to her, saying, "It's gonna be okay, princess, daddy's here," his voice cracking like brittle leaves. "I'm gonna make you all better, put you back together, and then we'll go for ice cream, okay, baby? Danni

Lynn, sweetie, talk to me. I'm right here. Don't worry, munchkin; Daddy will fix your boo-boo." His hands trembled so vigorously that the more material he tried to cup back into her head, the more he dropped. He cursed in a weepy manner every Time another piece fell from his shaking mittens.

A soft, mewling sound, like that of an injured animal, began to emanate from somewhere deep within him, rising in crescendo fashion until it reached the sonorous pitch of a full-throated, guttural scream of bleak misery. I did not know this at the Time. Still, after looking back and reflecting, I realized that his issuance felt as though it were directed at creation itself, a feeling and expression I did not recognize as coming from another human being.

I could feel the blood instantly drain from my face. I noticed the utter dejection on Mr. Reynolds' face as he turned to glance absently about the room for something unknown. His grim visage caused an overwhelming sense of panic, terror, and imminent danger to whisper along my spine, as though it were a hollow piece of bamboo, and to glide under my skin like some unctuous fluid. It quickly slid up my neck and caught in my throat like a fist, causing me to gag unchecked. The thought of dying at that moment made me not only retch on the spot but continue this sickly discharge as I broke for the front door, rushing Past Donnie without so much as a word, as Fear compelled me to seek refuge elsewhere. -

The revelation of this story herein is my way of expressing what the touch of her violent passing felt like to me. Even though I might not have been exposed to the actual threat of Death at the said moment, the feeling was comparable to what I now know the real thing carries with it. I Hope never to experience such a sensation again or be forced to contemplate the profundity of its insidious nature in my Life. The only exception I will make to this rule will be in relaying what her Death brought to me, how intensely it affected my sense of comprehension, and my desire to define its parameters for others, which I proffer herein.

The business of Death is an ominous motif for one to ponder. Its uncomfortable nature conjures forth a host of uneasy thoughts. Most people may need more confidence to contemplate such matters in the early stages of their lives, especially when it involves something that consumes their entire being. Most tend to relegate such musings to the recesses of the mind until they are prepared to address it at a Time when they feel more at ease contemplating its dour resolution.

I am one such person who has no desire to ponder it early on in my Life. It seems an unnecessary engagement for one so young, a matter I could postpone until the need to tackle it becomes too pressing to continue setting aside or ignoring. It will be kept for a Future date, as the young should not be troubled with such piddling abstractions of thought. Suppose this action proves to be in error. In that case, I will be forced to accept what may come and address it immediately.

Death may be an unpleasant subject for anyone to consider, but its concept is relatively straightforward to define. This relentless pursuer continues to haunt the steps of one's existence, the dogged shadow that refuses to rest and never gives quarter. The Fey truth about Death is that it is not an unjust measure, nor does it rob anyone of their fair share of Life. It is simply a state of finality, comparable to the last musical note in a score, or the final puzzle piece or clue that solves the enigma.

As noted in the previous paragraph, Death stalks everything in myriad ways. It confronts all Life at every stage of existence and is infinitely patient with the slow steps of its approach. However, with its advent comes a question that most humans may not have considered: "Could Death be that which spares humanity from this Life, or what condemns it to the next?" – (Philosophical perspective) Such a notion is an interesting prospect to ponder. Still, the problem with this type of ideation is that there doesn't seem to be a convincing answer to this query, at least not one that can bring any sense of peace or understanding to humanity's collective existence.

The reality of Death can elicit a gamut of emotions in those who become victims of its negative influences (hence the reaction in Mr. Reynolds). It can affect everyone differently, as its distinct resonance varies widely and depends on the number of elements in play. These factors can trigger a cascade of feelings that can lead to unknown physical changes in one's bodily chemistry. Such a mutation can significantly alter their state of being, their deportment, and ultimately manifest as physical maladies, which can cause severe distress or even lead to one's demise.

Despite Death's elementary design, there is no escape from its all-consuming touch. In no way should one consider its deployment methods restrictive or locked into a single actuation mode. There are many ways to experience the end of Life, and each aspect has its own means of enactment, independent of any other factors. However, such measures are subjective at best and relative to one's reckless nature, frame of mind, and situational Choice.

Despite my reluctance to admit it, I am guilty of being reckless at Times, unnecessarily coloring myself into a corner.

However, such is the nature of those who test the boundaries of propriety. Risk is sometimes its reward, as the essence one can pilfer from its result cannot be equaled in any other form. There is nothing wrong with contriving a little danger in Life, as long as one understands and accepts that, in doing so, they are standing at the bottom of a hole without a shovel, with no one to blame if someone comes along and begins to fill it, even though it is occupied.

Furthermore, I believe that the best way for one to meet their demise is by natural causes, specifically 'old age.' I Doubt anyone sits around hoping to curry such winsome favor, regardless of whether it is the preferable way to pass on. Could any manner in which one dies be regarded as a natural cause? The subtle difference implied here concerns the discomfort one might face in the final stages of their existence.

Consider the following list as it applies to how one might not wish to meet their end unless it suits their current state of being:

1) Suffocation.
2) Fire.
3) Disease.
4) Overdose.
5) Violence.
6) Starvation.
7) Suicide.
8) Freezing.
9) Hanging.
10) Bleeding out.
11) Electrocution.
12) Poison.
13) *Euthanasia.

*[The final concept in this list is regarding how much pain it may cause a loved one.]

The resonating question in my head at the moment is, 'If Death is so finite in structure (an immutable conclusion), how then can anyone ever Hope to wring happiness out of a Life that has been condemned since its origin, fated to be extinguished without pardon or reprieve?' It is hard to imagine any positive aspects arising from such a gloomy affair.

However, with the specter of Hope comes confidence. In the presence of such spirit, its beneficent manifestation will help breed Courage in the face of adversity, which is the definition of fortitude. Such a contrivance will cause even the most morbid predicament to gain ground and one day bear fruit, or at least that is what one can Hope for.

No matter the thoughts one may have regarding Death, humans can despise the act itself, even rage against it any way they wish. However, the one constant here is that no matter what its essence may bring, there is no real reason to Fear it. Death can do nothing more than what it is meant to do: end Life. What if humanity decided to look upon Death in a different light? What if, instead of viewing it in this frame of reference, humanity approaches it from a different perspective, one that reveals its cause differently?

Such a contemplative motif allows one to consider that the act does not instill most Fears regarding Death, but instead, how one will die. It is a known fact that most people Fear how they will die rather than the fact that it will transpire. The Fear of how one passes on is quite understandable, as no one wishes their end to be preceded by agony or pain.

However, this would raise the question: 'Why?' What would it matter? If one is ultimately going to die regardless of what they do, then why care how much pain one will be forced to endure? It is not something one will remember or be forced to bear with them in their passing ... or will they? Such a hypothesis is ridiculous to entertain, as there is nothing to be gained by its consideration. What will anyone care when they are gone?

In my experience, Death has been given a bad reputation by those who do not understand it or Fear it unjustifiably. With this thought in mind, the question should be, "Why does one Fear Death?" Such a quaere might be difficult to answer, as it tends to summon a litany of thoughts one would be forced to consider, leaving them without the quality answers they seek. Nothing in the world can seriously prepare one for what Death brings because no one knows what it will carry.

Consider why it is that humans have come to Fear Death the way they do. Is Death not an inevitable part of humanity's existence? Were we not born to die? This concept might sound strange at first, but it is undeniable. Death is an integral part of the cycle of Life, a natural occurrence that humanity knows will occur. The Fear one harbors in this context is a construct manufactured by rejecting the unknown they are exposed to and by things they disagree with, misunderstand, or refuse to accept as reality.

There is no logical sense to Fear a natural aspect or integral part of what one is. Such an indulgence will only hinder one from engaging in circumstances or affairs they might otherwise wish to consider or partake in were it not for the incessant nature of Fear itself. I would posit that the most effective way to counter the inevitable effects of Death on the mind is to come to terms with its essence. This will enable one to confront such a degree with equal gratitude, understanding, and acceptance, while doing everything possible to ease its unwavering approach and decisive delivery. "Death is a Time of reckoning, conveyed by the four winds, and liberated by the blade of Life's consummate emissary." – T.C. Monk

– PAST –

(5)

The word "Past" is a noun. It is defined as a combination of all things that have already transpired, that which has been completed, or something related to a former Time, place, or state of affairs.

***

One can only imagine how much of the Past they do not know. I will assert that what I possess of its complement is far less than what I do not. There are so many things I would be willing to surrender if I could be privy to the whole. My heart yearns for such knowledge. It would be a blessing to know the struggles of our Past, the defeats, the triumphs, and everything in between. But such is not to be, and I accepted as much as I humbly began to script this section. I understood I could only write about what I knew, the concrete truths I had been able to construct for myself, and what information I felt was appropriate or pertinent to impart to others. This bound me to a particular range of constrictive dissemination, as I have no wish to spread propaganda. It is a humbling realization that our knowledge of the Past is limited, and we must approach it with respect.

As I began putting pen to paper, I assumed this would be one of the more accessible subjects to script for this compendium, as I was familiar with its measure. I soon realized how much of that was hubris on my part and that this might become more complicated the farther I venture. I not only came to understand that the knowledge I had accumulated was incomplete in its own right, but also realized I needed to define much of it myself. Not the reality of it, but the overall conceptualization of its design structure. This truly irked me, as I was quite confident I knew its basic tenor before embarking on this endeavor.

With this newfound realization, my thoughts churned as I formulated this piece. To understand how the Past has been constructed, I needed to learn how it was perceived and how it should be highlighted for the reader. This was quite tricky and stress-inducing at Times, but in the end... all the comprehension I could glean from it was well worth the struggle for clarity. And now, as you, the reader, peruse this creation, take a moment to appreciate that it is a record of my Past, existing in your Present and preserved for the Future of all those who follow.

When pondering the streams of the Past, one may not realize how seminal they are to that which they have moved beyond. The Past has an innate quality that can help promote and improve upon any creative ideas and construct a workable path for Future development. This circumstance arises from creating a method for preventing Future mistakes—by recognizing those of the Past—and building upon its known formula for progress and success in the Present.

With this in mind, the author suggests that one should approach the victuals of the Past with a grain of salt, as nearly all of human history has been embellished and is only partially accurate. Some people consider the current documentation of the Past an accurate historical record. This assumption would be incorrect, as much of it has been corrupted beyond repair or credible use. In my limited capacity to debunk such discreditable narratives, the one constant humans can agree on is that all of their known history (their Past) was written and assembled by humans and adopted by them.

The portions of the Past that humans possess are not an actual record of true history, but rather a term I feel more comfortable coining as 'The annals of refined hearsay.' My case for this position is that history is often subjective, as the victors largely dictate its narrative. However, it is also assumed by those who were subdued by it and, after that, taught by individuals who are now subject to its written composition, which, in all actuality, is a form of cultural genocide.

The evidence for such a statement is not only based on the corrupt knowledge that most humanity has accumulated and accepted as accurate, but also stems from unconfirmed sources that document such false contrivances and Present them as facts. Nine Times out of ten, the information one acquires is second- or third-hand supposition, bound to how it has been relayed. No such versions of the Past can be identified as implicitly accurate. The only legitimate chronicles of the Past are those captured on film or by any other apparatus capable of recording it as it occurred. Any other version of history will have the scribes' and conquerors' shades woven into it. This is particularly true if one was not actually Present when the event(s) transpired.

Furthermore, it is impossible to control the vagaries of history or accurately correct its flaws. Great pains should be taken to secure its Future renditions—from this day forward—as there is no longer a need for propaganda war machines or the dissemination of misinformation to foster support or instill Fear. The only aspect humanity has to temper its judgment upon is the accuracy of such Past encounters and their relative interpretations.

It is a marvel how the human mind is equipped to record events it has witnessed. The fact that humans can do this for themselves, retaining it for Future review, is proof enough that their existence depends on these past experiences. It also rests in their ability to heed them with respect, especially if they wish to construct a Past of their own. Such an endeavor is necessary, especially when examining one's history. In doing so, one will be forced to draw from the mind's eye, as this is the only place it personally exists and can be summoned at will.

Consequently, when assessing one's memories of the Past, there is a strange elusiveness at certain intervals, one of its most frustrating aspects. This happens when one makes a concerted effort to summon specific memories from their Past, only to get lost in the shuffle or become absent altogether. This particular occurrence affects most humans at some point in their lives, and there is no way to combat it.

Another problem plaguing humanity is accurately and precisely recollecting events. Sometimes, the things humans believe they know need correction based on their memory of them. The basic structure of the memory is intact, but the details have become somewhat corrupted from their original state. An example is noticing something flash across one's field of vision. In this instance, the mind will attempt to process what it captured. It will knit together the details that it perceives to identify itself. If it cannot, it will try to extract what it can from its memory banks to piece together what portions it missed, thereby building a cognitive representation of what it believes it may have been. How and why this occurs is quite a mystery to most. Still, it is a solvable dilemma with patience and due diligence.

THE TIES THAT BIND

However, when one wants to reference world history, one must rely on either physical items collected from the Past or those that are part of it. The difference between these concepts is that one refers to an actual article 'from' a place, and the other refers to a written or recorded text 'of' an occurrence. Both notions involve Time, as neither could have existed without it. So, when one refers to or speaks of the Past, Time is a partner in tandem.

Albeit without a record of the Past to draw from, would anyone even realize Time or events have passed? And, if there was nothing for anyone to remember, would there be such a thing as the Past? Would it be something one even knew existed? No one can know if either circumstance is factual, nor can one dismiss it as nonsense. The Past is latent in one's memories, serving as a guidepost to direct one's Future endeavors. It gives one the confidence and control to strive for perfection in a world that is both warped and imperfect. Nothing in creation compares to the power of memory or its regrettable weakness.

Suppose humans recognize that the Past is based on humanity's limited existence. In that case, they might begin to understand how insignificant they are and how humbling this truth is. Despite this realization, one might consider how much of the Past has been recorded versus how much remains shrouded in mystery. If so, can one fathom which portions they have missed, the quality that remains, or the volume that has been hypothesized? Even if one could, it would be literally impossible to translate it into any quantifiable sense, comprehend it on a deeper level, or properly assimilate it.

The Past is relevant in both the Present and the Future. It is the aggregate content deposited into the library of one's own making. In this ecumenical setting, all things must eventually claim their own space, importance, and uniqueness. Here is where its bounty will be cataloged, given priority, and respected for its role in research and development, honoring the confluence of those who toil tirelessly to preserve its body of work.

In reality, the Past represents the best and worst of what humans have to offer, from a Time when their most significant accomplishments were shared with their penultimate failures. And, in this interstice, humans not only applauded themselves for both, but they continued making them on a grand scale, like nothing that may ever be seen again. But knowing humanity as I do, I Doubt this will be the last Time it will attempt to advance and ruin itself (and everyone around it), all in the name of scientific progress.

That said, humanity's Past is genuinely essential to Life. It proffers design, content, and reliability on an enormous scale, bringing clarity to a mundane reality. No matter what anyone may think, one should recognize that "Humans are echoes of the Past, voices of the Present, and vibrations of the Future." – T. C. Monk

– PRESENT –

(6)

The word "Present" (in its adjective form) is defined as the current state of being and of things in existence, occurring, or existing in the now.

* * *

In my desire to script this subject, I could not wait to sink my teeth into it, as this concept offered a space to fashion my interpretation of its reality. I was giddy with all the phrasing floating around in my head and burned up about half my writing tablet, attempting to jot down everything my mind could weave. But alas, I realized I could not use all I had slung down on paper and began mercilessly editing what was in front of me. It was a bit difficult at first, but the more I concentrated on the mess of content, the easier it became to weed out the chaff.

My understanding of the Present has always been that of a gift from the Future, a bounty for those who seek it. However, as I delved deeper, I discovered that the Future crafts a unique gift for each individual, tailored to their specific needs and level of engagement. This realization guided my decision about what to include and what to leave out, shaping my interpretation of the Present.

After the arduous process of editing, I was ready to Present my interpretation of the Present. I understood that while everyone has their own understanding of the Present, I needed to ground my interpretation in reality. The following presentation aims to clarify and spark curiosity about your personal understanding of the Present.

Firstly, the common understanding of the Present is that which reflects the Present moment. I found the term blasé, so I dressed it up and dubbed it 'The Shaper of current events.' So, to break the enchantment of the now, one must desire to move beyond one's captivating obsession with it and allow oneself to become an integral part of its progression. When one speaks of the Present, it should be with a sense of Hope and excitement for what exists while procuring a stable platform from which to enjoy Life's variety. No one can perceive what this will gain them or how it will come to pass, but such are the exciting reasons to chance reality and create a wild adventure out of the Present.

The now is unique in design. It presents the best available opportunities, allowing one to choose from myriad options to improve one's position. These opportunities allow one to gain an advantage in prosperity by applying keen attention to detail and preparation. It is through such measures that humanity will be able to gauge its success and pursue its continued existence relentlessly.

Nothing in the Present is lost on the morrow or yesterday, as it is both in the making. How one establishes oneself in each is contingent upon one's design for the Future and governed by the lessons of the Past. The position one assumes in this case should be geared toward establishing a gateway in the Present to create a roadmap that guides humanity beyond its current state and toward its next destination, while cautioning it about potential hazards along the way.

Regardless of the colorful references one can festoon the Present with, its overall concept has a strange sense of duality. Its structural motif suggests that Time is somehow related to one's location at a given moment and to the precise space one occupies. The connection between these two notions is subtle and often overlooked. One might not have considered both measures without knowing the definitions of the two concepts at play (Time and space).

The Present is a locus of confluence, a position of progress, and a bearing where Life becomes authentic. It is one of the constants in creation that does not vary from its intent: to leave its footprint, communicate its presence, and fulfill its purpose in evolution. It is a self-evident truth, a representation of Time's progression. This calculable movement is how one can perceive one's existence, measure it more comprehensively, and establish a point of reference to constantly track one's progress, growth, and place in Time.

Suppose one is capable of verily grasping this concept. In that case, it might go a long way toward revealing how everything in creation is connected on some level, a topic I touched on in the Life section of this work. Humans are a product of the same aggregate elements, born of the same fires, woven together by the same orphic forces, and bound by the same capital of law as everything else—Time!

The surreal thing about Time is that it is not only appropriate to the Present, the Future, and the Past, but also brings a particular benefit to their complement. Although each notion is connected to the other two (and to Time), each has its own method of application and usage within a specific configuration. It was contrived in this manner so none of these three concepts can affect, control, or dominate any particular aspect of the others. This is where the charity of Time, which I referenced above, comes into play, assuming its role as guardian. This restrictive measure is necessary to preserve continuity throughout the continuum of Eternity. One might wonder if it was an accidental affectation or a purposeful one. Such is a curious thought either way.

However, the Present exists to create the tapestry of the Past and the blueprint of the Future. The nexus between these abstract concepts makes them perceptible. Without this bridge, they would not exist. Humans would have nothing to gauge their experience, existence, or progress by, or even know that such measures exist in the first place. The Present is the definition of Life. It is the center of calculable existence, the yardstick of creation's muse. Humans should try to live only in the here and now, for it is the one component responsible for creating the requisite consciousness in all human beings. When humanity chooses to commit itself to such a station, it will be able to perceive its contrived reality and observe the visual universe more tangibly.

Suppose humanity continues to defer (to live in the Past). In that case, it will be relegated to simply existing, rather than designing a more beneficial way to live and thrive in the Present. Suppose humans are determined to focus strictly on the Future. In that case, they may lose sight of how to maintain what they currently possess in a positive, confident way, ultimately eroding who they are.

Herein dwells the Dream of what humans should strive for, rather than falling away from or hesitating about. Nothing in Life gets accomplished by those who do not challenge their Present in the face of the difficult, the unknown, or the risky, for rationality sometimes needs a more robust system to sustain its reasoning.

Humans should care more about how they interact with and treat their Present form of Life. It is the only one they may be afforded. It should not be squandered, taken for granted, or systematically abused by any measure of ingratitude, "For we are tokens of the Present, gems of the Future, and mementos of the Past." – T. C. Monk

– FUTURE –

(7)

The word "Future" is a noun. It is defined as the unknown events in the Future, a Time to come, and the condition of anything that will come to pass.

* * *

The feat of strength required to shape one's potential Future is a method that should be approached with patience and care. I found this utterly authentic as I began writing the commentary for this piece. Nothing can prepare one for the vast flood of thoughts inundating the mind when contemplating the Future. Its bounty is almost overwhelming at Times and boundless in its material availability.

After contemplating the parameters of its quiddity for a short Time, I concluded that my desire for its revelation was more important than the cumbersome nature of its constitution. At its outset, I was eager to write about the Future in a more existential sense, as I understood the essence of what needed to be scripted, just not how much would be involved in its presentation. The plethora of information available for one to draw from did nothing to allay my Fear of failing to Present it comprehensively and definitively. Although I recognized the content that needed elaboration, I needed clarification on where to start.

However, being my astute grunt, I leaned into it with both barrels and began to weave it one line at a Time. I accepted that this would not only be a very tedious and Time-consuming endeavor but a vital engagement in the overall scheme of things. Nothing would prevent me from conquering this behemoth and sharing the details I wish to relay with the reader. I had invested too much Time conjuring its material stock to succumb to defeat.

That said, please take a moment to absorb the contents of this exposé and allow yourself to ponder the profundity of what I proffer for your consumption. I attempted to keep its content within the navigational boundaries of logistical thinking and presumption during its scripting. I will posit that my recitation may be short and shrift, but rest assured, the contents of this compilation are replete with enough information to satisfy even the most diligent Knowledge-seeking individuals.

When attempting to unravel the obscure reality of the Future, one will struggle with its prodigious essence. The mean nature of its unscripted constitution is somewhat froward and restrictive, with its hidden content, especially toward those who seek its benefit without challenging the wheel of Fate. I firmly believe that there is no reward without risk, and absent any such challenge to one's existence, what measure of worth can one attach to Life in general? Life should be worthy of its struggles and hazards, or what is the use of continuing with its bourgeois grind? In this context, I find the words of A.J. Ayers quite poignant, "It seems that I have spent my entire Time trying to make Life more rational and that it was all wasted effort." How ironic is that?

The Future is an uncultivated realm of extraordinary possibility. It presents the most favorable stage for creating the Future self and augurs a hopeful future. In such ventures, the potential to conjure greatness from the seeds of mediocrity resides.

Here is where the womb of Time ultimately surrenders its bounty, paving the road for others with similar allusions of prominence.

When one speculates about the Future, it denotes a desire for more, for that mysterious essence dwelling beyond the spectrum of one's Time and energy, and does not spare much for the here and now. And, even though the Present is implied in its nature, humans need to focus more on preparing for what is to come rather than adjusting to what is in front of them now, as "The Future is the uncut chronicle beyond the moment." – T.C. Monk

What one hypothesizes about the Future often reveals a lot about them. It presents a wide assortment of Dreams one hopes to fulfill someday, along with a collection of others they know will never come to fruition. However, it is this blind trust in what humans are that allows them to be the true visionaries of Time and the raw craftsmen of their Future.

Most of the world's inhabitants believe in the Future, or at least a Future, but who is to say what this quality may actually bear? One can only Hope that the Future will produce a beneficial product that benefits everyone, although it doesn't always work out that way.

No one knows what the Future may bring or how it will manifest, but humanity can agree that there will be a Future. Now, how long this uncertain Future will last, no one can say with any certainty, as it is impossible to predict when it will end.

The Future is the unperceived realm of vast potential. It is the province where hopes and Dreams wager immense fortunes in anticipation of the odds being in their favor. However, when it comes to chance, these probabilities vary like the wind and are governed by the laws of averages.

With the promise of the Future being open, one can be confident there is ample Time for all things in one's Life. One must adopt patience in such circumstances to perfect everything in one's Life. This will Present an opportunity to excise any seemingly undesirable prospects (those not up to snuff) before engaging in any temporary or long-term investments.

When it comes to the Future, one must make the wheel of chance spin widdershins of misfortune to retain the benefit of its influence and keep the rules of eventuality at bay. The only way to accomplish this is to impose the focus of one's Will upon it with relentless vigor and chance, allowing only the most viable and beneficial opportunities to show substantial promise.

However, despite the Future being fraught with uncertainty, one must adopt a sense of hesitancy, as it applies to spur-of-the-moment assumptions to analyze them correctly before moving forward with undue haste. The Future is predicated on intuition and instinct. Many of our decisions are, at best, puzzling and leave much to be desired for self-professed futurists.

However, if one can solve the enigma of selfish suasion, they may declare their position in harmony with the Past, the Present, and the Future. This will enable the individual to become the weavers of their own destiny rather than their own demise. Such engagements can raise one's chances at the wheel of fortune and increase the odds of influencing the winds of change to blow in one's favor. This may well prevent the seeds of calamity from usurping any Future potential.

The best way to secure what the Future offers is to control the vagaries of the Present and the whims of the Past. It is not as unlikely or impossible a scenario as it sounds. However, one must be conscious that "The things we most live for must sometimes be left behind in the passing moments, or we will spend an Eternity struggling to retrieve the obsolete." – T.C. Monk

Furthermore, if one wishes to "Master the moments they live in - or for - they must not fall victim to the moments of the master." – T.C. Monk. This is the answer to the riddle of creation! Its solution reveals the symbiosis of Life, this being the communion of the Past, Present, and Future. As Shakespeare said, "There is a divinity that shapes our ends."

The only actual prospect humans have for the Future is to seek self-gratification, which makes it self-perpetuating. Anything that pleases the senses unequivocally comes from the physical world, so its continuation is implied. With the promise of Hope for tomorrow comes the threads of opportunity. However, in the absence of ambition, there can be no growth; in the absence of progress, there is no chance of success. The Future is all about imagination, productivity, and succession. There is no Hope without any of these factors.

Humanity's paradigm for Life is the struggle for perfection. Anything one attempts to accomplish in Life should be approached with the fewest flaws, as this is the Will of the spirit of conception. There is nothing more perfect than an imperfect creation. The little imperfections in beauty are what make a thing unique. It inspires humans to persevere and conscript them to be "Visionaries of the Future, historians of the Past, and ushers of the Present." – T.C. Monk

– DREAMS –

(8)

The word "Dreams" is a noun. It refers to the fantasy realm of the resting mind's contrived thought. Dreams also involve contemplating one's desires and aspirations, allowing one to turn these images into physical manifestations that benefit one's Life.

* * *

At the outset of this article, I envisioned many things that I felt spoiled for Choice, mainly regarding what I chose to include herein. There are so many ways to interpret Dreams, especially if those Dreams are beyond one's capability to actuate. I am guilty of this more than I care to admit. I have dreamed of marrying Jennifer Love Hewitt, tattooing Jessica Alba's entire body, and walking among the stars and unlocking their mysteries. All things that will never transpire, but such is the nature of a dreamer, to reach for, consider, or desire to have, possess, want, or need that which kindles the mind and is sometimes unattainable.

However, I will endeavor to script this subject within the boundaries of reality, rather than the wonders of fantasy. I hope that readers of this subject will gain a more concrete understanding of what Dreams are, where they originate, how they manifest, and what they can become. This includes the Dreams one might think are impossible to attain. Although unrealistic Dreams are those never meant to manifest beyond the mind, lest they shatter the beautiful illusion and leave one disappointed with the truth of stark reality.

After thoroughly contemplating Dreams, I have concluded that they are the unsung courtship between chimeric thought and kinetic execution. They exist within a boundless realm of divinity. Humanity's knowledge of Dreams is quite vague for the most part, as it applies to images conjured either by the unconscious mind at rest or by its consciousness at work. When delving beneath this obscure realm of possibility, one must be mindful of the numerous layers that reside here and the depth to which one can submerge oneself beneath its untold sheath.

The definition of having Dreams is to ponder one's ideas of interest and then nurture them to maturity with the least amount of damage to each concept. Here is where one can manipulate them at will (the daydreaming type) until they assume all the qualities and characteristics they were meant to possess before the first moment of manifestation in the mind.

To focus on the world of Dreams is to be conscious of what is in the here and now. However, one must be mindful of the beneficial aspects of one's Dreams, as only some things in dreamland are meant to be viable prospects for one's reality. Some Dreams are just random visions or phantasms of the mind. In contrast, others are more meaningful and productive models of reason, intended to be useful rather than a burden.

There are three types of Dreams humans experience:

☾

The first example is that of those with a factual basis and intended for real-world application. These specific types stem from what is known as daydreaming.

☽

The second example refers to what manifests in sleep, which occurs in two distinct forms. The primary of the two is that which forms while one is unconscious, as it proffers a pattern of ideas the mind can transfer into the real world, if they can be remembered upon waking.

☾

The third mode of secondary sleep dreaming is fictional, a manifestation never intended for actual implementation in everyday Life. Random images, such as these, are superficial manifestations of insignificance; however, sometimes these visual representations have genuine meaning in their cryptic displays.

The Dreams of sleep are a particular breed. They are Present in myriad stages of development and can vary, like diffusing light through a prism. These types of exhibitions have a multitude of meanings buried within them. Such revelations are complex and often confusing for those trying to interpret them.

Between these three types of fictive presentations lies the way the human mind—whether asleep or awake—reflects the physical desires in Life and indulges in them absentmindedly. Whether this is beneficial or detrimental is entirely random and unknown, and it cannot be easily influenced or managed without practice.

In the acquisition of Dreams, whether literal or figurative, within the realm of thought, one's true desires are revealed with purpose, intent, and substance. Such contrivances will evolve from simple fantasy into tangible objects with real potential for profit. Whether this advantage is solely personal or benefits others can only be determined by how the dream is constructed and by its purpose.

If one is patient and works to bring one's dream(s) to fruition with a specific aim in mind, such concepts will be framed with a sturdy foundation. This will boost their confidence to the point that they feel bold enough to take on any endeavor they might otherwise have hesitated to pursue. Here are the proving grounds of one's most daring enterprises, where they can be brought to fruition and completed with minimal alteration or personal cost.

However, do not assume Dreams are free. The scripting of ideas in one's head might be gratuitous, but the price one will eventually pay for their inception is one they will only be privy to once it is tallied up and levied against its recipient. Sometimes, the expenditure will be worth it in the long term and only seen as excessive once the damage has advanced beyond the point where amending or repairing it may no longer be viable.

When attempting to construct a comprehensive translation of one's Dreams, caution is warranted before taking any definitive actions based on the visions one might have. One should be careful with such measures, as any haphazard action may have unknown ramifications, especially those enacted without first attempting to discern the correct meaning behind them. Engagements devoid of such precautionary measures could spell disaster for the dreamer, particularly when one assumes their Dreams were meant to be literal representations of raw Hope rather than the figurative imagery of unrefined thought.

However, how humans construe such Dreams is up to them, as these visual constructs are bound only by the limitations they place on their imagination. Everyone's literal Dreams manifest in the mind like any other. The difference between the actual and the symbolic is that one has a valid application in the physical world, whereas the other is a crude musing beyond one's corporeal existence.

THE TIES THAT BIND

Some consider Dreams portals to the Future and clairvoyant revelations, and, in a fey sense, they are. However, these gateways of the mind sometimes reveal that not everything one conceives of has a place in this reality. The only conjurations to which one should give their undivided attention are those truly functional and beneficial to their Future.

Most people tend to shy away from or disregard this type of conscious recognition. However, these truths cause most individuals to lose sight of what is and isn't possible! It is disconcerting to witness the futility of labor being squandered on a hopeless cause, primarily when one invests all their resources in a single endeavor simply because the idea appears feasible in theory.

The struggle and joy of bringing one's Dreams to Life are a temporal process that can evoke overwhelming stress and profound relief. It is a curious and confusing process that fosters a Love-Hate relationship in the dreamer, who is the only one who can relate to it. Such measures are difficult to manipulate and to balance evenly, regardless of the effort one puts into their sphere of influence.

Anything of a dreamlike suasion should be handled with care. A limited amount is doled out to each person, and one should respect it. The dream state is the subconscious realm of creative thought and the province of unlimited potential. If humans are not mindful of relentlessly fostering their Dreams, they may one day find themselves without them. It would be unfortunate to realize too late that a person without a dream is likened to care devoid of emotion, which is quite an unfavorable situation. No one should lose their Dreams, as those are the fundamental components of who they are, what they have been, and what they could become.

With the veil of arcanum separating the playground of Dreams from the battlefield of reality, one must learn to fashion a bridge between the two, allowing them to convert the commodities summoned from the dreamland into something utilitarian and physically viable. As H.P. Lovecraft said, "Imagination is very potent, and in the uneducated, it often usurps the place of genuine experience."

Now, regarding figurative and unconscious Dreams, these capricious motifs merely symbolize enigmatic expressions to denote distinctive aspects of one's reality and how each vision manifests such fantasies. There is no telling why the mind cryptically reveals them. Still, for whatever reason it deems necessary, it is a measure one can only guess as to its polemic rationale. These types of Dreams require clarification regarding their true meaning and the nature of their revelation, but they are undoubtedly the mind's way of revealing humanity's sense of uncertainty. In reality, how the notion of such Dreams is interpreted will determine whether one advances or retreats from whatever labor or struggles humans face in their lives.

Why do humans worry so much about Dreams? Is it because they assume there might be a hidden aspect within them yet to be discovered? Is it a valuation that could lead to a sense of assumed entitlement, based on what the dream reveals? Or is it humanity's curious nature to puzzle out such problems that compel them to seek obscure answers? No one can be certain of the answers they would give. Although what humans can be confident about when it comes to Dreams is that whatever beneficial idea one can conjure for it, will be the literal dynamo feeding their desire for more Life. Nothing else can infuse the human spirit with such passion as a precious lifelong dream.

Personal joy stems from the Dreams we weave into reality. These desires fill the heart with happiness and joy, and humans begin to believe they can accomplish anything they set their minds to. Nothing in the world should prevent one from nurturing a dream in Life. Its very essence is autogenous, like the fires of the Sun, born from within.

Most Dreams have a specific purpose, but what that purpose is remains a mystery. The true revelation here is that no big or small Dream should ever be left undreamt, as all the world lives on Dreams. However, to hide them or leave them undiscovered is a lesson that can never be taught to those unaware that such fancies of the mind exist at all.

Being lost in one's reverie (daydreaming) works much the same way as sleep dreaming. However, when daydreaming, they can mentally modify and control the course of their reverie. This is in stark contrast to being in the sleep state, where one can only control or manipulate what occurs in the dream (to any significant degree) if they have spent Time learning to manage its domain. This state of abstract musing is where waking Dreams are woven into the things one fashions from such thoughts. It is the literal drawing board within the mind, where humans endlessly scribble, draw, erase, and reconfigure all they see in the mind's eye.

There is nothing about the realm of Dreams that is not manageable. Everything within is subject to the powers of the mind. All things are regulated and controlled by thought and desire. Nothing will escape its creative brush or the cut of its cruel hand. The capacity of its genius rests within the confines of its domain. It is only exposed by the touch of its master. Dreams are meant to be limitless and to represent the desires that abide in the heart, drawn from the infinite pool of inspiration and wisdom. The essence of such substances is measured by four means. The first are conjurations by the Muse of desire. The second are those channeled by the minstrel's spirit. The poet's mood influences the third segment. The artist's touch forges the fourth.

Every positive Dream should be capable of bearing fruit, as it is designed to be the figurative kindling to alight the soul, a means to assist humanity in its battle to triumph over adversity. And, in this contest of supremacy, it would be pertinent to remember that the essence of Dreams is a product one assumes from the shadowy province of undiscovered fortune and tends to retain the infirm nature of human disposition.

All humans Dream of tomorrow today, but does this sound like something other than the power of presage, especially if the Dreams of tomorrow are the whims of today? If this is the case, then humanity is living the Dreams of their Future right now, which makes them the dreamers of yesterday, the poor souls others poke fun at for being dreamers.

– NIGHTMARES –

(9)

The word "Nightmares" is a noun. It is defined as the artificial realm that constructs the most terrifying and haunting images, capable of evoking Fear. It is not only a graphic representation of introspective phobias causing humans to feel dread, but also anything that can frighten one from the unconscious activities of the mind. It is also a term that originated in Europe, referring to horses running at night. (Night Mares).

* * *

Trepidation and uncertainty harried me for days as I approached the topic of this section. The subject of Nightmares is not an easy concept to define or contemplate, as its very name conjures a chill from the depths of one's mind. Despite these feelings of apprehension, I endeavored to find the proper valuation to lend its complement and the suitable terms that could describe its nature to the reader. Once I finished formulating the plan for this subject, I decided to decorate it with a plethora of words and phrases that would lend strength, depth, and intensity to all the facets of its scripting.

My true intention for engaging in this type of versification was to inspire a sense of wonder and Fear in those who consume its verses. To touch someone else's mind with a passionately composed line is quite the tour de force. And, when it is actuated correctly, it is a marvel for those subject to its quiddity. Every person's engagement with my writing will not only differ from that of any other, but it will also manifest in myriad ways, one that may not have been anticipated or considered, in the form of presentational quality it can proffer them. My readers will likely experience every bit of what I intended to induce.

In taking on this harrowing subject, one dredges up thoughts of unspeakable experiences and visions of torment ravaging the world of sleep. Most images the mind conjures cannot be explained in detail, as they have no descriptive value one can apply to them, but they can be felt, nonetheless. These unfortunate plagues of the mind are relentless and quite disproportionate to the Life one leads. In a relative sense, this author would argue that they were unleashed from Pandora's Box specifically to cause humanity's consternation. Nothing else could explain such a ridiculous burden. (N.B. Do remember that not every issuance from Pandora's Box was negative. Hope did rest at the bottom of its vessel.)

Nightmares are troublesome annoyances. Crafting these terror-inspired visions leads nowhere and derives from the same nonexistent plane. How and why the mind weaves such horrors is unknown. Unless terror is its ultimate intent, there is no pattern or sense of meaning. The reason for such contrivances will confound humans for eons to come. Still, this author hopes humanity will one day solve the enigma for the benefit of us all.

Nightmares are the battlefield of the diabolical elite. They rule this realm unopposed, like a parasitic mob feeding on the frayed threads of human sanity. In this amorphous void, they can influence the ambiance and craft it into something so hideous and disturbing that it can provoke an ill-favored reaction in the body, sometimes to the point of immobility.

THE TIES THAT BIND

As intimated in the above paragraph, the mind seems to create these aberrations while at rest. The subconscious mind, a powerful and enigmatic force, may be at play here. The occurrence of such conjurations, latent and governed by prescient thought, could be a way for the mind to reveal something humans are either oblivious to during their waking hours or some coming circumstance(s) only the mind can discern. The mind's ability to create and reveal in this way is a testament to its complexity and power.

The world of Nightmares is a turbulent realm. There are no rules to its territory, boundaries, limitations, or mercy; it is a place where the unconscious mind creates and moves as it wills. It is a strange domain of visionary madness that conjures the raw Fears hiding among the myriad warrens of the chaotic labyrinth that is the mind. It not only crafts some of the most horrific visions imaginable but also allows one to ponder what they imagine or wish they could do, regardless of the consequences for others. Why such imagery dwells amid these unknown regions is most likely the id's way of taming the impulses humans Fear to engage in in the real world. It is also a haven where such terrible musings or fantasies can be brought to Life without risk or penalty to one's freedom, one's person, or one's inflated ego.

Despite these images being crafted in the mind, humans may need help understanding the vivid portrayals of each morbid representation and how they reveal themselves to a particular person. Each composition has a specific identity and distinct associative qualities, intended for perception. Nothing is left to chance or created without reason. One needs to puzzle out precisely what these things are to recognize how they apply to each circumstance.

However, there is still danger in this arena. It is not so much a physical as a psychological one. How most humans fantasize about someone or something else (morbid or otherwise) reflects what they may someday do. This is particularly true if they need to gain control of their moral compass and standards of conduct. Such musings may be harmless, but the more one allows such thoughts to rent space in their mind, the more likely they are to attempt to carry them out, especially if one's anger or infatuation gets the better of them.

Additionally, it is doubtful that all Nightmares are random. It is more probable that such contrivances are meant to be messages of some sort, hinting at the advent of some mysterious injury, malady, or unfortunate happening. These productions are more reminiscent of an augury, one denoting the arrival of something or someone at a fixed point in Time.

Most humans assume this is an innate quality shaped by the id, akin to a defense mechanism. It may also be those fey encounters most humans experience as Deja vu. The reason for this sensory perception is also an enigma. No one can say, indeed, why humans possess such an affectation, as there is no rhyme or reason for it, despite its presence in our lives. How the mind interprets and relays these visions is a mystery that will likely be debated for centuries to come.

Nightmares can also be the gateway to unhealthy thoughts, to that which sparks an inquietude in us all. They are the faithful, robed ministers of Fear and pain, prompting the mind to flog itself intermittently. They reveal humans are not only destined to suffer at their own hands, but they will also be forced to endure such injustice without quarter until their passing.

THE TIES THAT BIND

It is a strange feeling to sense the advent of punishment the next Time one falls asleep. This type of eidos can cause one to dread their impending slumber, sowing the seeds of apprehension and restlessness, almost to the point of mania. Such a state of disturbing vexation is an unfortunate reality for some people nowadays, as it has become an arena from which they cannot escape or find refuge.

This unfavorable result is a measure one must endure, like some inotropic tremors plaguing the terror-filled night. It is an unhealthy encroachment that breaks down the barriers of aegis and attacks one from all angles, like a pack of feral dogs. But such are the wages of Fear exerted upon those who script their worst reality.

Everyone has Nightmares, and these experiences affect us all in myriad ways. No one is immune to its intricate web, nor can they dismiss its sinister touch as easily as they make it appear. Some folks are more adept at hiding the things that terrify them, what strikes Fear in their heart, or what makes them weak in the knees. However, boxing things up this way is no easy practice. It takes Time and patience to learn how to categorize such afflictions of the mind and render them into moments of simple irritation.

The implications of these particular visitations are potent enough to enlighten anyone about what Fear is, especially if they have yet to experience it firsthand. This is how one can genuinely comprehend absolute terror without actually suffering it. Such an engagement may help temper one's feelings of dread and apprehension in the presence of its lingering echo, particularly if one can learn to master the moments one lives in, rather than live in the moments of the master.

Now, there is no arena in Life where Nightmares are not the rulers of the stage, thespians of the art, and force their quarry to endure the cruel renditions of their impious tragedies. And, even though they are performing such scenes in the theater of one's mind, it is to this literal gallery that humanity has become forever bound to suffer beneath their ministrations. The weavers of these dreadful visions of horror represent the unlimited reservoir of unbridled savagery dwelling in the bowels of the human mind. Its aggregate force is commanded with ruthless abandon. It exposes the infernal bounty in what this author coined "The unruly domain of self-terrorism."

– VIRTUE –

(10)

The word "Virtue" is a noun. It is defined as one having or possessing the right or desired qualities of moral excellence. It is a trait that stands out above all else simply because it does not fit in just anywhere.

* * *

As I began framing the work for this section, I hoped for a measure of simplicity in defining its station's parameters. At first, I was intimidated by the thought of attempting to define the essence of its quality—my interpretation thereof—but the further I traveled across its gamut, the less it harried me. I was relieved that developing its overall structure came much more easily than I had anticipated.

I was intimidated by the thought of defining it for others, because everyone's concept of what a Virtue is may differ from mine. I had no desire to be castigated for being presumptuous or insisting that it be bound to a particular frame of reference without a modicum of flexibility. Such an insinuation would have seriously boxed me into a corner and woven a shroud of pseudo-hubris around me, one that was unsolicited, undeserving, and unintentional on my part. Please understand that whatever notion the reader takes away from this creation is their interpretation of my presentational rendering.

See it as one may: Virtue is the highest status among our species. It is a surreal thought to accept, but the fact is that other human beings created Virtues. They were not a set of tenets handed down by some omnipotent being. They only exist due to the resolute nature of a particular class of individuals who sought to establish the standards of equality and the balance necessary to maintain such a grade. By this measure, humanity can reach the pinnacle of its existence among its peers and make it a permanent home, one we can all be proud to say we live in.

When delving into the core of this concept, one must recognize that it deserves respect in its own right and is primed for mass adoption if deemed worthy. One should not chance the wheel of worth-ship here, mainly if unprepared for a severe Life struggle. The avarice blade tends to bite deep into those who fail to measure up to the quality of virtuousness and those attempting to skirt or misuse its edge. It will leave them with the bitter taste of failure stuck in their craw, a most unpalatable sensation one may never rid oneself of.

Despite the difficult hurdles one must overcome, the topic of Virtue is quite interesting to consider and investigate, as its substance draws upon one's curiosity for moral rectitude. It is not easy for anyone to achieve such a state, yet it is even harder to attain. The strict mental discipline required to achieve its rank and file is almost comparable to asceticism, which is only a practical undertaking meant for some. However, if one can weather the storm and diligently fight for what they wish to achieve, they might just reach the top of the ominous mountain looming before them.

For the clarity of those who may misunderstand the spectral composition of such traits, Virtues are not mutable compositions, nor are they subject to whimsical alteration. They are a superior set of strictures, fixed in their constitution, that govern our species' personal and professional conduct. Every Virtue set in stone carries guidelines to regulate its boundaries of decency, much like the DNA in our bodies.

The uniqueness of Virtue resides in its creation, whereby it proffers one the best chances for personal development. It is not a prospect that one should fiddle with insouciantly, but a practice meant to be studied and applied to the self, much like the requisite tools of one's craft. These traits are by which humanity gauges the quality of others and measures its own worth. Virtues can also be related to one's skill sets, ones that are based on a particular set of grounds by which it is measured, such as: *by, or ... in Virtue of (meaning - owing to, thanks to, because of, on account of) – [*Oxford Dictionary.]

Furthermore, at one point in the Past, Virtues were meant to represent status among society's factions. Virtues dictated how one spoke, how one was spoken to, and the style in which trade and business were conducted, with a simple handshake, one bereft of worry or distrust. Through these degrees of Virtue, our society has established the embodiment of perfection among humanity, solely through sheer determination.

Virtue is the epitome of purity and goodness. It does not allow its quiddity to be wielded like a scepter if one does not own the same quality or character it represents. It takes great control to command the essence of a Virtue, a strength from someone worth their salt. Anyone can possess it, but only a fraction of folk can employ it correctly. Such is what makes the traits of Virtue so coveted by others who do not possess them. It takes dedication, discipline, and determination to incorporate these qualities into one's arsenal of distinction. The great pains one takes to imprint these qualities upon oneself can only be revealed when one is put through one's paces. Only then will they veritably know the cost of Virtue.

The following list should provide one with an idea of such disciplines that exist:

1) Honor

This aspect should reflect one's ability to uphold specific standards of conduct toward others and to apply them when acting on their behalf.

The first example concerns how one treats another person, such as someone who lacks a particular skill, has a debilitating affliction, chooses an alternative lifestyle, or any other situation that leads them to believe they can set themselves above others.

The second example speaks to the manner of one's conduct in the name of another, such as fighting for someone's dignity or Virtue, an obligation one assumes for another, an oath made to kith and kin (or any other person), bearing witness for another, caring for the elderly, or any variation of such actions.

All such engagements fall under the class of Honor, one not only subscribes to but also wishes to be known by and has preceded them in all aspects of their Life. (See the 'Honor' section included herein for further details.)

2) Courage

When it comes to the definition of this aspect, it sets a heavy toll upon those who seek its quality. Every facet of this notion is intended to instill confidence in those facing adversity or uncertainty in Life. Courage manifests in myriad forms and affects everyone in a slightly different way. Still, the baseline of its quiddity will always remain the same. (See the 'Courage' section included herein for further details.)

3) Loyalty

This aspect doles out the essence of its bounty in a particular way. The nature of its existence is evidence that not every human can be trusted, or why would it exist? Under its umbrella fall every engagement one might partake in, whether toward another or the self, as its employ is the same, and this is to instill trust. (See the 'Loyalty' section included herein for further details.)

4) Love

Oh, how does one count the shades of Life's consummate mate? It is unbelievably difficult to script everything for this aspect. I dare not attempt to do so as I might lose myself in its tangled web. Including every variation of this multiphasic Virtue would require more space than I am willing to allot here. However, I will include this tidbit for the reader: L.O.V.E. is the 'Links of Varied Elements' that bind all facets of humanity together. – T.C. Monk [See the 'Love' section for further details.]

5) Justice

This subject requires an understanding that its essence varies depending on how it is applied and administered. Justice carries a multitude of subtle shades to its tapestry. Every person believes they understand the true nature of justice. Still, I would say that everyone's notion of its definition is colored differently and utterly depends on their circumstances.

I wrote a poignant quote back in 2002 regarding this Virtue: "Justice is a sign of true equality, one that promises no immunity but that which we grant." I stand by this sentiment, as the only ones who can summon justice's hammer-or pardon its stroke-are those it truly affects.

Justice cannot be the blade wielded by another, nor can it be sought and meted out by anyone else. Justice cannot be satisfied by another's hand. Such a ridiculous sentiment must have been crafted by a masochist, one who enjoys inflicting pain on others for their own twisted pleasure. If an individual desires justice, it should be theirs to seek and acquire, for if it is good enough for anyone else to collect a pound of flesh on another's behalf. It is good enough for anyone to collect their apportionment.

Justice veritably belongs to those who were unjustly violated, pure and simple. No one else has the right to make another pay for their faults with their bones and their flesh, especially if the violation did not involve them. The only Time such action should occur is when one is unjustly deprived of their freedom or their Life, and only if the individual is no longer Present to seek reparations for such a personal violation. My thoughts conform to the maxim, "Seek and levy not upon another, lest it be sought and lofted upon thee." – T.C. Monk

Justice is the fair and equitable treatment of every person, regardless of who they are, where they come from, what they choose to do in Life, or why it was created to begin with. As I mentioned earlier, not everyone will view it the same way, nor should they, as each person has their own definition of justice. The true measure of equality is to see and do what one may, in any way one chooses, and not be dictated to or shamed by another's point of standing, especially if they think they know what is better for another person, despite the individual's wishes or desires. (There is no other section on 'Justice' in this work. One can find its relative connections under 'Loyalty,' 'Choice,' and 'Honor.' Its relation can also be located in section #9, Integrity of this section.)

6) Patience

I once read a profoundly posed query on a sippy cup that belonged to my two-year-old niece. I believe it was a 'Dennis the Menace' cartoon rendering; it read, "Mom, why does 'in a minute' take so long?" What a marvelous line and a perfect sentiment to begin this passage. If I only had the patience of Sisyphus, I would not mind how long '...in a minute...' ends up being. However, such is not the case. It took me years and a great deal of blood, sweat, and effort to cultivate the level of patience I now possess, and I am grateful for it.

It is said that 'Patience is a Virtue.' Ha! Whoever coined this must not have understood the level of stress it breeds in those it afflicts and probably never sat around waiting for a swimming pool to fill or paint to dry. The following quotes best define patience: "Patience and delay achieve more than force and rage." – (La Fontaine) and, "Sorrow and silence are strong, and patient endurance is godlike." – (Longfellow)

Has patience ever lost patience with itself? Hmmm. Regardless of the fun I poke here, I realize patience is a necessary Virtue. I can only say that with its addition to one's repertoire, it will go a long way toward sanding down the burr in one's saddle and the deadening effect it has on one's mind.

To have patience means to bear the weight of whatever troubles one's current existence, to weigh it on oneself, and to seek something else to focus on while awaiting its inevitable passing. (There is no other section on 'patience' in this work. One can see its relative connections under the 'Faith,' 'Courage,' and 'Choice' sections.)

7) Hospitality

This altruistic concept is simple in its definition and application. It is an action every person must learn to proffer and accept as a gift to and from another. Initially, it is not something one must earn, like respect, but a matter of being grateful for its creation and availability, rather than the alternative. No aspect of this notion can harm anyone or cause them to suffer unless the giver intends harm. If this is the case, such an action would fall under the headings 'Hate' and 'Treachery,' two separate sections in this compilation.

However, one must be cognizant of those they are hospitable to, as anyone who is undeserving or attempts to take advantage of another's generosity (kindness for weakness) does not deserve one's grace. In this instance, one must demonstrate their worthiness to receive and retain such fellowship, or they will not be granted such a gratuity in the Future. Showing and receiving kindness is the mark of decency in any human being. If one cannot be decent, be gone with your shabby self!

8) Duty

Such is the mark of the noble, the principled, the virtuous, and the reason it falls into this grouping. It is challenging to define duty for others, but most understand it as what one must fulfill. Be it a requirement made by oath to someone else, to the self, or in another's stead. Regardless of which identifier it carries, it binds one to the fact that they have set their word upon if they are honorable.

When it comes to one's duty in Life, one should assume a position that allows for Honor. One must always be sure to say what one means and always mean what one says. If one cannot adhere to this simple quality, they should not open their pie hole. It would be better to keep one's mouth closed and play at infirmity than open it and remove all Doubt. I heard it said once, and I am paraphrasing here, "One must be careful of what they say, lest their words become trapped in the amber." – (Kurt Vonnegut [Quote variation]) [This work has no other section on duty. Its relative connections are found under the 'Honor,' 'Courage,' and 'Choice' sections.]

9) Integrity

The idea of this subject refers to one's conduct. Their actions reveal their character and sense of rectitude, whether in the presence of others or when alone. This is reminiscent of H.L. Mencken's statement, "Conscience: the inner voice which warns us that someone may be watching."

The best description of integrity is the one that sets one apart from the average person's reaction to a particular situation. This will require a strong sense of Will, especially if the act affects someone else's Life, their social circle, or those they interact with, as it alleviates a great deal of insecurity about their intentions and Future actions. (There is no other section on integrity in this work.

One can find its relative connections under the 'Honor', 'Loyalty', 'Truth', and 'Duty' sections.)

10) Truth

I cannot stress the importance of this subject, as I defined it in the section entitled 'Duty'. One's word should mean everything, have a pith to it, and relay the same concreteness to those who hear it, rely on it, and are affected by it. The truth should always be the fountainhead for conformity to fact, as the damage it can cause otherwise is unknown. Thomas Mann penned it quite nicely when he wrote, "A great truth is a truth whose opposite is also a truth."

However, I heard a profound truth that elevated this concept to a new level of reality. I'm trying to remember who said it, but it came from a television program; I can't recall its title. I will paraphrase it here: "The truth is a matter of perception and, at best, subjective. It is winnowed through the sieve of our personal experiences and shaded by our biased observations." – (Monica Raymond [TV series co-star])

This revelation gave me much to think about, and after considering it, I decided its interpretation was correct. The overall message I took from it was that one person's truth may not be another's. Strange as it sounds, it is an axiom (a self-evident truth) that cannot be disputed. How anyone sees any particular thing depends upon their vantage point, perspective, and relative perceptions. (There is no other section on truth in this work. Its close connections are found under the 'Integrity', 'Honor', and 'Choice' sections.)

This may seem like a short list of disciplines (10 in all) to absorb and put into practice, but such a thought would be a grave error. I could have gone on for a Time with the definitions of these characteristics. Still, there is no need for such a measure of personal investment in a particular practice that benefits others more than oneself.

The fact is, Virtues are positive influences in anyone's realm of existence as they promote a better character quality. It is the manifest destiny of the noble, the righteous, and the humble. Nothing in the world should be capable of swaying such an altruistic impetus. Just think about how the qualities of such Virtues (in their entirety) could resoundingly affect any actions in Life. This endeavor should be the staple of every human being on the planet. It would be a more beneficial, more productive world to live in if we could abolish crime, poverty, politics, and senseless Death altogether. If one were to adhere to the Virtues listed herein, there would be no reason to employ such engagements.

The trouble with Virtue is that once a person experiences its influence, they crave more, almost to the point of nausea. It becomes like an infectious scent, a substance one craves more of because of its effect on one's emotions. The nature of humanity is sensory-based. It is driven by its constant need to know (taste, touch, hear, see, and smell) everything within its calculable existence. Without such reasons, why would anyone wish to continue living if they cannot attain what they desire, become a part of its cause and/or effect, or be consumed by it? Are these not the reasons to live? If not, please thrill me with your acumen... I am all ears!

– VICE –

(11)

The word "Vice" is a noun. It is defined as any form of evil or immoral conduct. It is (to some) a defect of character or behavior propagated by wicked or corrupt learning.

* * *

The thoughts swirling through my mind when I first began to shape this subject were varied and provocative. It was interesting to ponder the Vices I have wanted to engage in but have not, because of the stigma and aversion most people attach to them. However, the ones I have dabbled in were quite interesting and pleasurable. I am sure this is the inevitable outcome of engaging in such forbidden impulses.

I have always thought about engaging in various types of safe play with my female partner, such as whips, ropes, candles, blindfolds, and role-playing - being either submissive or dominant - depending on my connection to her. I think it is essential to experiment with one's significant other. Life is about pleasure, and pleasure is about testing one's limitations in a safe environment and with someone trustworthy. We all have fantasies we wish to indulge in. Still, Fear of the shame that may come with it prevents most from engaging in such taboo experimentation. Why I say it is essential to experiment with one's partner is to show them you are not only willing to be vulnerable and open, but that you are also amenable to letting them be free to engage and express their feral side (without judgment), the one they have been starving for far too long.

Pain is not really my thing, but I have come to understand that the types of pain capable of eliciting pleasure might be an interesting concept worthy of investigation and indulgence, if only for knowing the stimulative qualities such actuation can yield. There is nothing wrong with trying something exciting or new, especially if it can be beneficial. The concept of being at another person's mercy is a fantasy most people have; they do not openly voice such flights of fancy for Fear of judgment by others. However, its eidos can have a seriously enticing effect on the mind, a force or sway that has no equal in Life and is only constrained by one's employment and tolerance. To know how another will treat you, or how they will allow you to treat them, is an intoxicating elixir for the senses, a kind of philter for the mind.

Why such a factor exists in our species is quite a wonder. However, I think it has more to do with how much pain, humiliation, and/or discipline one can or is willing to endure before saying "Uncle," which stirs the embers of curiosity in one's mind. Consider how such engagements relate to the following statement: 'The test of one's resolve is a staple that most everyone in our world partakes in, a desire to pit their Will and endurance against all others. It is not only the Hope of success or victory that pushes humans beyond their limits, but also the willingness to risk failure and defeat, which drives their instinct to prepare for any challenge. Such is the competitor's heart and passion, and what resides in their Will to stave off defeat. If not, why would one's vaulting ambition to be 'the best in the world' even be an issue of contention?' – T.C. Monk

The rigors of this exposé may be genuinely bothersome to most individuals in our society, but somewhat of an enticement to others. Its essence does not conscript everyone into its cult of personality. Still, it does summon the worthy, the curious, and the vain. However, nothing in Vice is easy, as every notion has a particular valuation. No matter where they are employed, which reminds me of a quote by Pascal: "The heart has its reasons, which reason knows nothing about."

Initially, Vices were not meant to be engaged in by just anyone. It is genuinely troubling how humanity abuses Vices as it does. These particular indulgences were initially established so that an afflicted person could explore the dangerous, the unusual, and the taboo in a safe environment and at a controlled volume. This was primarily due to the dangers it could pose to the uninitiated, the naive, and the unprepared. Not every person is ready to be flogged or trussed up like a tent in a closet. The fringe folk of society often engage in taboo activities, seeking something more challenging and thought-provoking than the established parameters of mainstream culture. This author posits that most people nowadays recognize the true nature of Vices, that they are primarily a pleasure the readied mind can enjoy, and only if one is truly prepared for the unknown. If one elects to indulge in any particular discipline, one should do so with caution and moderation.

Vice is a venal contract. It exists at someone else's expense, or for one's own satisfaction and ego. No matter which Vice one decides to partake in, its ultimate goal is the gratification of the self on an ascending scale. For the most part, the key to this is temperance, and even though a Vice is considered an act of evil or immorality, one person's repulsive sin is another's indulgent delight. (The following quote by Shakespeare sums this sentiment up quite nicely: "There is nothing either good or bad, but thinking makes it so.")

The benefit of Vice, however, is its ability to adapt and become flexible (overlet) for those who desire more out of Life than boorish contentment. It is an engagement to instill a sense of freedom from captive oppression. It is used to bury one's pain or smother sorrow beneath a shroud of euphoria. It may also be a method to compel them to the point where their fantasies can be transformed into a state of pleasure - whether shared or alone - if only for a short period. This is somewhat valued in what Somerset Maugham said, "Excess on occasion is exhilarating. It prevents moderation from acquiring the deadening effect of habit."

Just about anything one partakes in can be considered Vice if it is viewed or tagged as taboo by society's powers that be. Such strictures are usually imposed by those who object to anything that might offend their delicate sensibilities. The eldritch thing about such sentimentalism is that it is introduced, practiced, taught, and restricted by one's predecessors and those who publicly oppose it. Such activities are not only subjugated by individuals obsessed with setting the tone for society, but also by those who privately engage in such prohibitions! In this case, I would venture to say, "What is good for the goose is not good for the gander." – (idiom. US.)

To most people, this is no surprise, as the concept is based on the institution of guilt by suggestion and application. However, certain proclivities are fundamentally detestable and should never be practiced or tolerated by anyone, such as the abuse or exploitation of a child, sex trafficking, dismemberment, etc. These taboo subjects are not simply objections imposed by others, but rather a natural aversion to such notions that promotes their acceptance and engagement.

THE TIES THAT BIND

Consider the following list of practices that fall under Vice:

1) Murder
2) Prostitution
3) Theft
4) Greed
5) Drugs
6) Alcohol
7) Perversion
8) Cruelty
9) Deceit
10) Gambling

Such a list may seem manageable, but it can be deceiving regarding the variations within these Vices. Each of these practices requires a personal and financial investment from its user to elicit the desired results. The need to alter one's reality comes at a cost, and the piper will not waive the fee for anyone. When each person decides to foot the bill, it will depend on how much of a modification to their reality they require and for how long.

Keep in mind that Vices are not meant for everyone. Each has a specific clientele it caters to, nourished by its intense and versatile nature. The issue with this type of conscription is that once an individual is exposed to its stimulant for a particular amount of Time, they will start to crave more and need more until it becomes an internalized desire. And, even though Vices are mostly indulgences of the moment, they tend to become habit-forming in those who overuse or abuse them. Used in moderation, such a practice cannot rise to the point of serious injury but can create a physical and psychological dependency within the practitioner.

Furthermore, its continuation must be maintained when one becomes a victim of such effects. If not, the feelings of euphoria sustaining them will begin to dissipate and usher in the symptoms of withdrawal. This contretemps stems from the absence of the essential ingredient needed to help the body suppress its feral cravings. Without such a suppressive substance, there would be nothing to protect the participant from suffering needlessly, becoming sporadically violent, or acting irrationally to satiate the pain of need.

Most Vices harm those who partake in Excess. Everything about such indulgences can become quite malignant and spread like wildfire. The more it is fed, the stronger it becomes, and the less likely one is to escape its grasp. There is nothing positive about Vices unless one enjoys being miserable under pressure, delights in the pleasures of pain (to the self or another), or has the requisite desire to test the boundary of one's acceptance and tolerance.

One can consider Vice any way they wish, but it is the most potent lure one will ever encounter in Life. It will draw one in, seduce them, entice them to use again, and dare them to be bold and rebellious. Vice never relents in its mission to recruit new participants or previous users. It is a savage beast that cannot be tamed and does not know defeat. One could spend a lifetime in its wicked clutches and never escape or know peace.

The only influence one can wield over a Vice is the power of abstinence, but this, too, will be a constant struggle to maintain. Its resistance will be tested at every turn, by every measure, and in any place one may attempt to seek its refuge. However, when one least expects it, there will come a Time when its stamina will fail in its support (no matter how much one fights) and again cause one to fall victim to its specious melody.

Now, when it comes to the different Vices that exist - for males or females - these will vary in degree, application, and necessity of the moment. Each individual has a unique need, desire, or want that satisfies their particular craving(s). No person possesses the key to the perfect formula when engaging in any Vice, as each has its own equitable valuation, tailored to the individual.

When it comes to Vices, most are simple and tend to fall into three categories: Addiction, Sex, and Boundaries. These three topics cover the Vices most people engage in throughout their lives. I may not define every single one here, especially regarding females, as their issues are particularly complicated for me. Still, the ones I need to clarify for the readers will fall under these three definitions.

1) SEX

(a) This subject is complex for most males to touch on, as none of them want to come off as perverts or degenerates for desiring the things they do and are afraid to vocalize such for Fear of being shamed or judged by those around them. The engagement of sex (speaking for males only) is a little more than a basic need for the immediate release of pent-up stress or energy that they cannot release any other way. And yes, this means by any means possible, whether through the assistance of a willing female, personal engagement with the self, or, unfortunately, by force. For a male, a female is perfect for this act of initiation, depending on how intensely she is willing to let him pursue her. (The film's first part, 'Savages,' exemplifies this perfectly.)

The first two descriptions in the above paragraph are straightforward and the usual course of acceptable activity;

however, the latter, 'by force,' is troublesome, as its use varies from situation to situation and still falls under the same premise of control. Typically, when a male sees a female he desires, rather for partnership, to mate with, or simply as a means of release, he does not initially consider her feelings at that moment, nor her want or need of such unwanted attention, nor does he, unfortunately, mark her age as a measure of consideration.* At the outset, his desire is simple: to have her for what he requires, nothing more, and she would be willing to accept such a proposition if she only understood his primal need for her. *(Within reason, for age-conscious males with moral standards.)

When it comes to age as a factor for sex, there is a teetering scale that marks it for each individual. It differs significantly for each person, shaped by how they have been taught what is acceptable by society's standards. In all honesty, younger males seek older females for sex knowledge. In contrast, older males seek younger females for unrestricted access to what they are willing to give up. The younger ones primarily seek financial support from older males.

In contrast, older females often seek younger males to groom and care for, often because of their vigor and perceived virility. (Sometimes, one needs a bit of the rabbit to satiate a need.) Consider where the world would be if anyone had objected to King Ferdinand of Aragon's decision to marry Queen Isabella of Castile at such a young age. Remember to consider all the other females who were instrumental in shaping our history at such a young age.

Today, such a manner of thinking is frowned upon and considered vile and criminal. Most males are taught to be a bit self-centered. Their primal thought is not to harm the female in any way - unless he is mentally ill - as most males crave/need/

desire a female's touch more than they will admit. The male wants and needs it to be administered of her own free Will. To him, if he can attain it, it is an aphrodisiac stronger than any drug in the world. Empires have crumbled and been razed to the ground because of the desires of a single female. However, the more the male focuses his cravings on her, the more he mentally screws with his moral compass and his sense of right and wrong, the sooner his animalistic nature will turn against itself. This action will eventually lead him to consider attaining it by force, no matter how much his mind objects, especially if the woman turns him down, slights him in any way, makes him feel unworthy, or is out of his league.

All of these factors are what create the situation where a male will fall into an undesirable state of physical violence toward a female he wants or needs at the moment. Some women do not realize how their words can affect a man in such a fervent state. Or how far he is willing to go if he feels degraded, especially if he begins to fancy knocking her down a peg or six to teach her a modicum of humility or respect for someone stronger than herself. A woman could be more mindful of how she dismisses a man, particularly in a more considerate manner, without provoking his ire.

Now, yes, some males do not know how to take dismissal appropriately and continue to hound the females. Many males perceive this as playing hard to get, a behavior often taught to us at a young age. Such an active indulgence is a practice braided into the fabric of our culture and something females should not only attempt to recognize and understand but take delicate care to temper their dismissal of any male, such as, "Hey, this is not me playing hard to get, I am just not interested in being pursued, but thank you for the compliment." It is not that hard!

Now, I know this will only work for some situations. Still, it will cut down the overall hurt feelings females know they inflict on males, which they dismiss inappropriately. And yes, the female's job is to be mindful, firm, careful, and confident. Not every male will be violent, no matter how a female chooses to dismiss them, but being prudent is necessary at every juncture for consistency and safety. It is sad to say that females are forced to police themselves and respond in a certain way, but it is in their best interest to do so for safety reasons. It is a measure by which they can legitimately control their immediate surroundings.

Sex for a male is different in many ways from that of a female. Most males take it as a simple form of enjoyment. In contrast, the typical female (if there are any) mostly wants to engage in it for procreation. However, they also derive enjoyment from it. Still, from my deductions, such is not their primary focus, especially if they are family-oriented. If they are not, they tend to assume the male form of engagement for the pure sense of satisfaction and bodily enjoyment. Such an engagement is acceptable on all levels, despite society criticizing them for being promiscuous, which is an antiquated form of thinking meant to control women's attraction to every other male except for those who set the rules.

When it comes to sex with females, I think of it in a particular way that some females may agree with and some may not. My ultimate engagement when it comes to sex is not to add another notch to my bedpost, but is more geared toward wanting to share an experience with the particular females I fancy. I want to share myself with them and Hope they'll feel the same way, understanding what that experience could bring to both of us.

From what I have deduced over the years, every human wants to experience as much as they can in Life. Still, they loathe being criticized for their desire or wish to engage in the taboo subject society has tagged as lecherous, immoral, and sinful. I want to experience everything possible with every female I can, and I Hope she or they may wish to do the same. Life is meant to be explored and enjoyed for the pleasures it can conjure for each of us, separately or together.

2) Addictions

(a) The general topic I want to touch on for this section is any stimulant the body can experience. The term 'Drug' can denote anything that can affect the body to the point where one will need more of its essence to sustain general functionality (just as outlined in an earlier section of this article) without causing significant physical damage to either its male or female participants.

A drug/stimulant doesn't have to conform to or denote a particular physical substance, such as a prohibited liquid or powdered element (whether refined or not). It can be any stimulant that affects the mind in the same manner as a typical drug might. Sex is one of these afflictions, but so is gambling, any adrenaline-inducing sport, visual stimulant, physical sensation, as well as any manner of sensory perception not generated naturally by the body.

Any of the above selections can induce such a state; the strength of its effect on the participant, how its substance transforms into the desired euphoria, and how long it lasts, all depend on these factors. The longer its effects can be sustained for enjoyment, the more one will desire its quiddity again, thereby seeking it out at all costs, despite the detriment to Life, liberty, property, or the self. I cannot stress how important this factor is. It has almost an equal impact on someone as the equation for 'surrender gains power,' which is what a female does when she surrenders her body to a male to gain control over her Life, if she truly understands how to wield it properly. This is why dominatrix play is so powerful for both males and females. Surrender is power, and it is a drug!

It is the same with gambling. The power one relinquishes to the cards, the dice, the wheel, the stats, etc., is how one surrenders power and control to the laws of averages, hoping the odds are in their favor. This allows one to think they have some control over destiny, even though it is a pseudo-essence. Such is a guesstimate based on an assumed former assessment and an average statistical probability, which only sometimes pan out as one calculates or bets on. This is the specious lure of the game, something one can chance their luck against on a whim.

The same applies to adrenaline-fueled activities, sensory experiences, visual pleasure, or any other indulgence that may induce enjoyment for the mind and/or body. There are many such things I could not include here, not only because the list is too extensive, but also because each person's indulgence varies in degree and intensity. What I mean by this is that the intensity level will be different for each person, as will their Choice of activities, their desired Time of engagement, and each person's comfort level and measure of acceptance.

3) Boundaries

This particular frame of reference targets activities involving Life-altering pressures, such as war, protecting one's Life, the lives of family and friends, and personal possessions. The list of boundaries for the individual is essential not only to them but also to each in their own way, and to them retaining the same valuation, regardless of what that particular thing happens to be. Every person's boundaries are set by what they are willing to sacrifice for and how highly they value it compared to other things in their Life.

For example, a car may mean everything to one person, yet mean nothing more than a mode of transportation to another, something to which they have no other attachment. Anything humans attach a semblance of value to will be particular to that person and not subject to anything beyond. For instance, some women will protect a specific possession more than their own lives, such as a wedding ring or family heirloom, whereas others will not. It ultimately boils down to what each individual is willing to sacrifice.

Boundaries are essential for all of us, not only those set by society's leaders and socialites, but also those we establish for our personal spaces, livelihoods, and spheres of sovereignty. All of these subject matters are worth fighting for, even unto Death, especially if one fancies one's measure of peace, a sense of freedom not only for one's kith and kin, but also for the society in which they live. Sodalities cannot continue to exist peacefully without appropriate boundaries to limit one's interactions with others, whether their own or those of another culture.

Boundaries have allowed our collective societies to continue to exist despite those who relentlessly seek to undermine them at every turn, particularly when it doesn't suit their needs or cater to their whims. Unfortunately, this will not last, as the powers that be are bent on destroying what they can no longer control, which is another boundary in and of itself. In the grand scheme of things, we humans, as a race of sentient beings, will sometimes elect to destroy our excess rather than share with those having less than we do or with others deemed less worthy than ourselves. Such is not a law of nature but a measure that human beings have instituted to determine those who deserve it and those who do not.

Overall, humans have chosen to relegate other humans to poverty despite all of us being family in one way or another. We are all children of Mother Earth, grandchildren of the stars, and scions of the universe. Humanity should come to understand that the boundaries we set for ourselves and others are those that genuinely limit the potential to be more than we think and verily retards the ability to be progressive in its most genitive form.

With this thought in mind, it reminds me of a short statement I wrote about worth-ship: "I believe that any human being should not have to prove they have the right to draw breath, to be free, to count for something. However, I believe every human being should recognize the right of another sentient being to exist and be allowed to decide what it does for itself. We should not judge each other based on the altar of public opinion. The persistent need for what we are and what we wish to be will be reflected in our decisions regarding how we treat and judge one another ethically, no matter the cause ... especially if any such action is designed to hamper or strangle one's right to live." – T.C. Monk

– CHOICE –

(12)

The word "Choice" is a noun. It is defined as having the power or opportunity to choose between two or more options. It allows one to be selective based on one's personal preferences, Choices, or alternatives, instead of being stuck with what remains.

* * *

I will begin this section with a fabulous phrase by Joseph Conrad: "The mysteries of Choice, scented like a flower, quiet like Death, dark like a tomb, and uncertain like Time." What a ridiculously scripted phrase. Few writers can weave a sentiment like this, let alone infuse it with a definition that mirrors its theme so keenly. I must tip my hat to him.

This subject was a joy, as it allowed considerable latitude in defining its interpretive frame. This benefit allowed me to experiment freely with the conceptualization of its parameters. Such is the guise of a writer, though, getting to craft what they feel into something someone else can perceive in the theater of their mind. However, one must be cautious of what one writes, as it often tends to lend itself to a one-sided view if one is not mindful of how one's scripted intent could be interpreted. It serves as a reminder of the importance of being mindful of our choices and how they can shape our perspectives.

Choice is not just a concept; it is a pathway to personal growth. It is a prelude to the Future woven into the Present. Engaging with this subject, one decides to learn more about how to draw from the probable to create the compatible. It is a concept that inspires one to move forward and create a path to where they desire to be, rather than remaining content with where they are. This concept has been a transformative experience in my Life, and I will be forever grateful for the Choice I have, as not everyone is afforded such a benefit in their own lives.

Now, I want to clarify that Choice is not just a calculable component in Life. It is a meticulously structured element that enables humans to choose how they engage with a series of options. This scale allows one to select from the remaining options based on the number of probabilities (a prefabricated path). It then permits them to devise the best plausible Future one could Hope to achieve.

For those who are uncertain, Choice is finite, not infinite, and measured in degrees. Most people believe it is driven by personal preference (the lesser of two evils) rather than by some unseen force. It is an engagement one must accept or refuse by default (a forced decision), which seems more akin to testing one's resolve than to allowing freedom of choice. Whereby does one become comfortable or feel safe engaging in such if one's Future is bound by election and not natural selection? The differences between these two properties define the measurable distance between Choice and Fate.

Consider this: to live (once born) is an option for every person, and in each moment, choosing to live beyond that moment is a decision to move into the next phase of one's existence. The Choice is simple: they can either move in any direction or pass on; there is no other alternative. A decision must be made so that the pattern of one's Life can continue in whatever direction it may. No one knows why this is an option, but it is an interesting concept, especially if one chooses the Life cycle rather than its companion, Death. The inevitability of this Choice, the weight of it, is what truly defines our existence.

Furthermore, suppose that Choice is humanity's way of controlling. In that case, it should not be restricted to a particular allotment when considering options beyond the selections. Each possibility should be geared toward the benefit of that specific instance and what might profit or aid in developing the uncertain Future. Each selection should only be relied upon as an aspect of advantage or gain if one knows all the angles of its measure. To do so without certitude would be tantamount to forcing one to deal with and accept what comes by happenstance rather than by personal design. Our power lies in the design of our own choices.

Upon pondering this revelation, it no longer carries the same appeal it did before I understood it. My questions would be, 'Why should humans feel the desire or need to opt for such decisions, especially if Life was never a Choice at the outset? Might this be due to their inexorable wish to know more? Or, humanity's infirm nature to be more than what they are that compels them ever forward?' In whichever manner one views such a concept, it is a circumstance humans have become tethered to like a moment in Time, one they are bound to by its irrevocable nature.

With the number of options available in Life, one is sometimes spoiled for Choice. However, suppose fortune is the favor in humanity's existence. In that case, they should be grateful that a Choice exists, even if only a single option is available. The reality that humans possess the privilege to select from those presented is a gift in and of itself. And even if one refuses to choose any available path, they are still making a Choice, as the decision not to choose is an avenue of adoption as well.

Allow me to illustrate for clarity. Say, for instance, one is standing at a crossroads. How many options are there to choose from? Is it four? Is it five? Six? It's five. One can go left, right, backward, forward, or stay put. The final option depends on whether one is putting down roots where they stand or is only there temporarily. If it is the latter, one will eventually be required to choose an alternative path (a forced decision). People cannot fly, so up is not an option, and digging a hole will get one nowhere.

Furthermore, such a range of available choices is evidence that something among the cosmos devised it in such a fashion, dare I say, 'Intelligent Design.' If this is not the case, there would be no choices; only a linear path would exist, with no variation. However, this also denotes deliberate design, as it exists precisely because it is there as a Choice.

The thing about the number of paths traveled is that if one stays the course long enough, they will eventually intersect with the initial site where their journey first began, especially on this planet. This concept holds even if one's path is curved, meandering, twisting, curling, or spiraling. Every single path leads back upon itself in some manner or another; such is the circuit of Life design and the eventuality of it coming full circle.

So, what does humanity do with the guise of Choice? Should they believe it is predetermined? Should it be seen as some luck of the draw? Or, chalk it up to what one creates for oneself? Who answers these questions is up to each person. No one can know what the truth is for anyone else. Humans can hypothesize what they believe is the ultimate truth, but it will always remain a mere guess.

Could it be the path's end that humans undoubtedly seek, making the journey worthwhile? It may be the risk-versus-reward aspect one wishes to tempt oneself with. Perhaps the danger posed to one's Life is what one wishes to gamble with, making it interesting.

Or, it is the unknown factors along the way that prompt them to move forward, those veiled experiences humans may miss out on if they choose the wrong path. T.S. Eliot regretted not taking another path when he wrote, "Footfalls echo in the memory down the passage which we did not take toward the door we never opened into the rose garden."

It is impossible to determine which of these unknown factors influences humanity's decisions. It could be one, all of them, or none of them; there is no certainty here. However, no matter which method it turns out to be or how many, humanity will indeed engage such eidos by its leave and be confined to them by its own thoughtful decisions.

The choices humans are proffered in Life seem to be inextricably bound to five distinct measures, which are:

1) What type of Life does one desire?

2) What, and how much, is one willing to endure to achieve such a Life?

3) What, and how much, is one willing to sacrifice to obtain the advantage they require?

4) What, and how much, is one willing to share with another?

5) What, and how much, is one willing to endure alone?

Such contemplative motifs are strange to consider and ascribe to one's Life, but they are nonetheless true in every position. There is no argument against forming these five themes, as each applies equally to everyone. Otherwise, why should anyone desire to continue with such a jaded reality, especially one full of adversity, hardship, and pain? Aren't such reasons what drive humanity to test its limits, to strive ever forward? Do these tests of what humans are willing to endure, sacrifice, and share with those they choose to have in their lives make it worth the struggle? I see no other legitimate reason one could apply to it that would lend it any more constitution than this.

Be that as it may, the devil is in the details of all realities of existence. Humans interact the way they do based on learned practices from their predecessors, especially when choosing what they need or want at any given Time. Everything one elects to have in Life should be applied toward the betterment of oneself and those around oneself, particularly if one desires a profitable Future with like-minded people. So, one should actively participate in scripting their Choice, lest someone else do it for them. The decision is ultimately ours to make!

along for the ride as an observer, not an unknown variable that could upset the delicate balance.

So, the question is, does this revelation make Life worth living? Does this make it a bit unbearable? Does it even make sense to consider? Or are humans simply indifferent to how it will turn out? Surprisingly, it is both a yes and a no. How is this? Well, the "yes" portion of this concept depends on whether one cares about how one will die. The no factor is based on the reality that they will die regardless, so why care how it transpires?

To some, it is important how Fate approaches them. Suppose they can tweak the path offered (just a touch). In that case, they can forestall Fate's hand a little longer, enough to help pilfer some of what they are not entitled to from somewhere else if possible. The unwavering passion to cheat Death is intense and desirous at all points, and a matter that most humans desire to find clues as to how this can be made a reality.

However, Fate makes no allowances for variation in its Web of Life design. So, no matter how hard one may try, there is no relief from what cometh, no quarter, and no do-over. If there is such a redo, then it would no longer conform to the threads of Fate but the colorful strands of Choice, those beholden to the laws of averages. We already know how the grade of Choice is governed, as revealed in the section titled "Grade of Choice."

However, most people have accepted that one cannot change one's Fate and have resigned themselves to that reality, enjoying what they can while they can. This sentiment is echoed by Darrell Royal: "[Fate] is what happens when preparation meets opportunity." There is nothing wrong with this type of engagement except when such interactions interfere with the Fate of another, especially in ignoble ways.

In the grand scheme of things, humanity should question: Is Fate actual? Is it essential that humans should wish to control? Should they Fear it? Should it be ignored? Was it meant to be tinkered with or influenced by those with malicious intent? This author would intimate that one should never try to modify it nor allow it to be consigned to or manipulated by humankind's unbridled, reckless hand. If one truly has a Fate in Life, it should remain unsullied.

It is not conceivable that the final query in the above paragraph could be a reasonable answer unless the architect of Eternity wishes to sample - and be party to - all the evils of creation. If this is the case, what more do humans have to look forward to? How much more will humans be forced to endure for the sake of experience? It would be loathsome to imagine the extent of such an endeavor and what it is that desires to absorb the essence of such pernicious acts. This would give rise to the ugly thought that the architect of Life is malicious.

In a world chock-full of possibilities, the ticket to free Will does not appear to exist beyond the idea of it. There is no reason to believe this notion about Life, as destiny holds all the cards and plays them accordingly. However, what if it were possible for humans to alter or manipulate Fate? What then? The question here is: Can Fate be influenced by force? Or, will it remain steady if one does not meddle with it in what this author defines as "Competitive engagement" or "Selective Choice?" Considering this subject, carefully ponder how the following tale supports such a position.

- The story of Moses (Moshe) and the rock -

God (YHWH) told Moses (Moshe) that when he arrives at this particular rock, he simply speak to it, and it shall bring forth water. When Moses finally came upon the rock, he did not talk to it as instructed but struck it with his staff, and water came forth. Was this an act of 'Selective Choice' or 'Competitive engagement?' Did Moses do this with the intent to disobey? Was he predetermined to strike it? Was it Fate that caused him to hit it rather than speak to it? Was it even a Choice? Or was it an attempt by God to influence Moses and dictate, change, or control his Fate?

Was this a command by God or a mere suggestion? Was it to test Moses, to see if he would continue to obey? If it were, then God does not know all (mirroring the Garden of Eden story). But if it was neither of these options and Moses was fated to strike the rock, then God not only knew what Moses was destined to do but also attempted to influence, change, or control his Fate and punish Moses for something he was predetermined to do. If God did not want water to come from the rock, Moses' disobedience could not have altered that decision.

Sure, one could argue 'Free Will' here, but if Fate is set, then 'Free Will' is an illusory concept, as there is no free Will if one cannot genuinely affect one's own Life. It would be a moot notion in every sense and has no business in the same conversation as Fate. However, if one believes that God granted humans free Will to choose because He loved them, then why was Moses punished for exercising the free will He was given? And, if God invented or controls free Will, then what is the use of having free Will to choose if God can alter it on a whim or punish us for deciding to employ the blessing of free Will we were granted from the beginning?

Such a contretemps would leave anyone pleading for grace. This would imply that God wishes to dictate parts of humanity's existence (a slavish mentality), not one with the freedom proffered to it or the Love God supposedly granted them. But how can this be? Humanity is taught to believe that God loves them and that they are to multiply and replenish the earth. What benefit would this bring if humanity were conscripted to order? This would be like ordering fast food from a drive-thru, or like a blueprint of our genome, made to order, shaped for a specific purpose, and not meant to deviate from that course.

Humanity's belief in Fate's parameters is not concrete. Evidence of this can be gleaned from the following maxim: "A belief is a manual to deceive oneself, one wrought on the anvil of obedience." – T.C. Monk. The truism behind this statement is that all the information humans consume was entirely contrived by someone else. These were their thoughts, ideas, and reflections on creativity, not everyone's reality. What humans subscribe to is their Choice, not something chiseled on a stone tablet taken from another culture.

Think of it this way: if one were born out in the wilderness, alone, with no books, no one to teach them about the world, what it has to offer, what it can force-feed them, would they know anything about percentages? Would they know what a God is? Would they know about Fate, Love, Faith, trust, betrayal, or shame? No, they would not know any such perceptions humans have manufactured for themselves. All of these, plus numerous others, are man-made concepts, societal constructs, and identifiers that have been woven by others and assumed as fact by the masses. This is the furthest thing from the truth, as such ideations are merely matters of perspective and a means for the mind to attach a tag to for Future recognition.

So, any concept humans ascribe to is nothing more than one person's fancy or caprice, a thing they find either beneficial or practical for their Life and/or stimulating to the mind. Although this overall theme is in keeping with the idea of Fate, Choice has given humanity enough room to experiment with it, to the extent that they are stripped of reality and tend to rely on a crutch to help them along. One can speculate about what might have happened if they had chosen another path, but the idea is moot and diminishes their intellect.

According to the measure of Fate, humanity's Fate is already set, and no one can alter it. How one colors their tapestry is entirely up to them. Although not in a fashion that will allow them to dictate their placement among the mosaic of Life. Humanity's novice hands may develop the colorful additions, just not the essence of its overall design, as this lies within the sole domain of Fate. Despite all of humanity knowing the end will arrive, we must recognize that none of us has a Choice but to wait for its inevitable advent.

– HOPE –

(14)

The word "Hope" is a noun. It is defined as the blending of expectations and desires directed toward a person, place, thing, idea, or circumstance. Hope is an expression of longing or craving for something one wants, Dreams of, or has an ambition for. It is a measure one uses to count on or trust in what one seeks, even if it is not a fact.

* * *

Hope is often touted as having a profound impact on humanity. However, I have not found it particularly effective in any aspect of my Life. Relying on Hope has never brought me anything of value, as it is not a tangible thing one can perceive with the senses, but rather more of an idea woven around one's Life. It is a peculiarity that humans engage in not only for mental support but for the benefit it can bring to the hearts of those who believe it is real.

Sometimes I have hoped for certain things or wanted something to turn out well, but nothing came to pass. At one point, I believed that Hope possessed beneficent powers for each person, a particular substance that could help them acquire what they sought. But then, I began to learn about Life, became educated, and realized the truth. It was a humbling experience, especially when I discovered that Santa Claus, the Easter Bunny, and the Tooth Fairy were not real. All these revelations were cold shots to the ego, and I wanted to castigate my parents for introducing such nonsense into my Life.

I do not harbor any ill Will toward them for such fabrications, as I know they meant well and were trying to pass along the traditions they were exposed to. However, instituting such false contrivances is unnecessary to the overall structure of the human experience, as they tend to teach young people that lying is acceptable as long as it does not harm others. These are not only the first instances in which children are exposed to 'little white lies,' but also their primary exposure to betrayal by a loved one—maybe not an intentional betrayal of the heart with ill intent, but one of the mind. I felt betrayed when I found out they were all fabrications grafted into our lives from other cultures' belief systems, especially Santa, as this one was used to try to keep me in line. Grrrr! It could have worked better.

No matter the reason, Hope is part of humanity's existence. Engaging with this theme requires relinquishing control of one's life and replacing it with belief in something they desire to be true. This subject gives one the sense that, no matter how hopeless any predicament appears, with enough Faith in something beyond what one knows, one can overcome any desperate situation one might find oneself in. This is absolutely false, and it may lead to their demise if they bank on it to save them at the most inopportune Time.

Fear, Doubt, and Despair nurture Hope. It is the one intangible no one could have planned for, nor realized how intensely it can motivate someone beyond what they assume is possible. This product is one of consolation, an Eide remaining after one loses their conviction. It is also a sentimental affliction affecting those who need not only a crutch to reinforce their resolve but also the strength of mind to support their uncertainty and a component to help them cope in Times of unpredictability.

Humans use Hope not only as a tool to build and strengthen their confidence but also as a product to help them muscle Past the obstacles and demons holding them back, discouraging them, and causing them to Fear something they do not know. Its existence is meant to bring them a sense of comfort and a measure of warmth. However, most people can only maintain such a quality with its benefits, as its presence is something one can lean on while searching for their true purpose in Life. Now, whether this purpose is positive or negative is quite a mystery, and no one will be capable of discerning this until they make a Choice as to what calls to them.

Furthermore, even though humanity has carved out a place where Hope dwells as a constant staple, it does not mean that it is the governing factor for them or something they can influence. If it were possible to shape one's Life with Hope alone, the world would be a much different place than it currently is. However, since such an endeavor is not plausible, humanity must Hope that Life and the rest of the world will get better sooner rather than later.

The purchase of this quiddity is vital for all aspects of one's being. It can strengthen a person's resolve (as stated previously) and force them to move forward and persevere, particularly in the face of uncertainty, dejection, sorrow, desperation, and Fear. It is also a transcendental method of adopting one's mental vision, which reflects the design or prospect one chooses to pursue. It allows one to extract the unknowable from the improbable, helping one believe in the impossible.

The overall sentiment here is that Hope is more potent than Fear. Fear can prevent one from engaging in or changing anything in Life. It can even cause them to act irrationally. Hope will provide one with a reason (a measure to reap results) to push forward and confront their Fears, thereby allowing such afflictions to be faced with Courage and conviction, regardless of the risk to oneself. The following quote is apropos of this: "Fear is a strong stimulant, but Hope will compel one beyond the anticipation of misfortune." – T.C. Monk

The accent of Hope resides within the precise nature of one's proximity to danger or Despair. Its manifestation proves its existence, thereby highlighting the current pressures it faces. There can be no argument against this, for Hope resides everywhere, even among those who have never met. To understand this much is to know where Hope begins and Fear, Doubt, and Despair end.

Consider the following quote by Shakespeare: "Hope is a flatterer and a parasite." This is one of the most meaningful quotes I have ever read, and it could not be expressed more clearly or more truly in any language. I will also include a quote I penned years back: "Hope is a shield against the darkness surrounding humanity daily. It is a sense of trust, a belief in something more than the self. It can offer one the impression that every situation is not hopeless." – T.C. Monk

The author created the following axioms (self-evident truths) to help define Hope's essence in its most expressive forms. These personal expressions are intended to elicit a cascade of emotional and thoughtful responses from the reader.

1) Hope is a passion inspired by the Muse, a charm of making crafted by you.

2) Hope is a flame that warms without touch, like a diamond that sparkles from every cut.

3) Hope is the essence of the Sun and Moon; it infuses our souls with its copious hue.

4) Hope is a feeling beyond all need, the strength to persevere from somewhere deep.

5) Hope is the charm to enchant the melody, a song we craft within our memory.

6) Hope is a smile that imparts care, a gift to enjoy without judgment or Fear.

7) Hope is a gift we must protect by fashioning hymns into prayers that bless.

8) Hope is the candle that burns in the heart; it fashions the Dreams upon which we embark.

9) Hope is the eyes that wish for more, the desire for aplomb that leads to valor.

10) Hope is a weapon to defend the heart, to banish the demons we craft in the dark.

11) Hope can be cultivated from the tiniest seed and manifested in Dreams in the world of sleep.

12) Hope is forgiveness without a crutch, a remedy that can heal even the deepest cut.

13) Hope is the meaningful mystery solved, like the joy we capture from the rain that falls.

14) Hope is a ballad born of threnody; it springs from a child in constant reverie.

15) Hope is the comfort within the flame, an intimate shroud to ease our pain.

16) Hope is an ocean of a thousand blooms, each one nurtured by the strength within you.

17) Hope is the essence that makes us shine, like a fluorescent sunset, capturing the eye.

18) Hope is a delicacy upon the air, like dandelions, whispers, and blown kisses of care.

19) Hope is a desire that touches our core, like the gift of light from a distant star.

20) Hope is gift-wrapped in a child's eyes, like the Moon at night, to reveal the tide.

21) Hope is a warmth we all can feel, a shared secret only the lover reveals.

As one can extrapolate from these sayings, the sentiment of Hope runs deep, and as Alexander Pope said, "springs eternal in the human breast."

– DESPAIR –

(15)

The word "Despair" is a noun. It is defined as the complete absence or loss of Hope.

* * *

Most people would say they have experienced Despair at some point in their lives, just as I have, and that it can have quite the effect on one's mind and body. It can also take a heavy toll on those in one's circle of family and friends, especially when they see how much one is suffering and they are helpless to console them. I have been in this position many Times, with no one to lend a favorable word or a shoulder to lean on, but I managed to work through it on my own and am much stronger for the experience, despite its lingering effects.

Despair has many facets and shows no remorse or compassion for its victims, nor does it care how they suffer. This undesirable prospect can strain the mind and body to the point of exhaustion. It is not an aspect anyone would want to experience, as its symptoms can be severe and stressful in numerous ways. When one is unfortunate enough to experience its essence, the strength by which it affects them will differ significantly. Its influence will depend not only on the substance that first conjured it but also on that which continues to feed and compel its resilient nature.

Myriad things influence humans. At Times, it appears as though one may thrive on this type of negative pressure, as it tends to inspire a measure of confidence based on how much one can endure. This can only be attributed to one's personal preference and the need for a spur to promote progression in one's Life. I can relate to this concept, as I have a strange affinity for pressure, stress, and conflict. It tends to bring out the best in what dwells beneath the surface static of my being.

Despite needing a crutch to force me to think outside the box, I have found that if I manage the pressures well enough, I can find my safe place. However, I have been forced to step back at Times due to my inability to manage it, almost to the point where, had I not, I would have become a victim of its influence rather than its puppeteer. A forced interaction made this manifest with people whose pressure threshold was more significant than mine, which is rather difficult to accept for someone of my caliber.

Despair is not an aspect one can summon like the feelings of Hope or gratitude, but rather an essence manufactured by the mind. It is a symptom of failure and hopelessness, one that blankets the conscience like a shroud, blocking out all of the external influences that could potentially alter its current state of suffering and infection. The more one thinks about it and contemplates its substance, the worse it will plague its victim. No one is safe from its insidious touch.

There is no immediate relief from Despair, as it seems to have its plan. The types of afflictions emanating from its substance are diverse and interdependent, and should not be dismissed or treated lightly. They are hardships that can completely break a person's spirit, leading them to act irrationally and disregard their own safety and that of others. The length of such an imposition may be tethered to the stamina of one's own Will, and if left unchecked, it will wreck almost anyone. If it does not ruin, it will snuff out.

Furthermore, if someone is currently suffering from its effects, its essence has already had Time to germinate in the mind and take a firm hold of its target. Once this occurs, it may take years to rid oneself of its corrupt and negative influence. As intimated above (regarding stamina and will), one can learn to manage one's longevity and its impact on oneself. Such a measure, however, is a complicated endeavor, and something they might want to investigate further. The actual methods of control or treatment may end up making them worse, maybe even encouraging suicidal tendencies, which is a whole other beast!

No particular affair can corner the market on how or where Despair may arise. Its essence can stem from various sources, including the loss of money, a pet, a job, a friend, a lover, or myriad other Vices humans allow themselves to engage in. Its residual touch can alter mental, spiritual, and emotional states and dramatically affect physical health. The physiological response it can elicit is capable of conjuring a cataract of sensations, such as sorrow, dejection, grief, depression, and many others arising from its unfortunate substance.

The nature of Despair is not an aspect anyone should allow to fester inside them. It is a deathly silent killer approaching from the depths of one's being. If one can recognize the effects of Despair when it hits, only then will they be better equipped to battle its quiddity. Consider the following three quotes as to how they correspond to the essence of this topic: "To Hope is to live with the fruits of Despair." – T.C. Monk. "Happiness is beneficial to the body, but grief develops the power of the mind." – (Marcel Proust), and, "Sorrow is tranquility remembered in emotion." – (Dorothy Parker)

– FAITH –

(16)

The word "Faith" is a noun. It is defined as having complete trust or confidence in what one believes or knows, especially without logical proof or absolute fact.

* * *

When I first began crafting the details of this piece, I was somewhat conflicted about its overall concept. I understand what it is and why it exists, but its reality is not based on a theorem (provable science) or anything truly tangible. Most people might argue this point, but their disputation would ultimately be futile, as there is no evidence to support the notion beyond their own contrived reality. They may pose no way of disproving it, but the point is that one does not need to prove its nonexistence, as the only fundamental aspects of Life can be established. Anything outside this measure is simply head fog.

I say it in this manner because most people connect Faith with religion, which is also a concept that does not exist beyond what humanity forces itself to believe or subscribe to. Regardless of the number of plausible arguments one could manufacture to support such a position, there is no way around this fact. I am not knocking what others wish to place their trust or Faith in, but just for clarity, what one engages in is nothing short of self-manipulation. If this is something particular people need to help them through their lives, then so be it. However, I would ask that they refrain from imposing their beliefs on others, from convincing others of their own truth, or from criticizing others for not conforming to their beliefs.

That said, I will impart that Faith derives from a sense of needful connection to a substance beyond what is known. It compels one to continue seeking that unknown essence outside the natural order of one's being. This endeavor is multifaceted and tends to afford those who engage in it considerable latitude at its inception and throughout its ongoing development. And, the amount of conviction one imbues their Faith with will determine how much it affects their Life. Something must feed Faith, as it does not exist without reason. It is not a genuine need but rather a measure of want.

Faith has only one parameter: trust in that which one cannot feel, see, hear, touch, or consort with the physical sense. Sure, one could pose this question about prayer. Still, such is not consorting in the real sense humanity knows it to be, especially with something more than themselves, an entity they Hope exists and will hear their emotional entreaty. With this thought in mind, I would like to include a brief excerpt from another article I wrote years ago, titled "Unreasonable Insanity." The parameters of its revelation center on human creative theory and include the concept of contrived Faith.

- The word " unreasonable " is an adjective. It is defined as going beyond what is necessary or proper, being irrational or illogical, and being unwilling to be guided by sound judgment or equitable conduct.

The word " insanity " is a noun. It is defined as being affected by madness or a sense of lunacy, being out of one's mind, taking leave of one's senses, or assuming things beyond one's reality.

THE TIES THAT BIND

The term Unreasonable Insanity refers to one's inability to be reasoned with or reason with oneself in a reasonable manner. This is a particularly aggravating engagement, especially when one knows the path they have chosen is fraught with pain, uncertainty, heartache, supposition, and Death. Laurens van der Post explained this with utter clarity: "Human beings are perhaps never more frightening than when they are convinced beyond a Doubt, they are right."

If there exists one place in the world where every consciousness pursues the same common interest, it is undoubtedly in the silence that stills the soul. In the moments when one seeks to be noticed by something greater than the self, humanity has a limitless connection with one another. Here, in these instances, humanity should question whether it is genuinely worthy of the quiddity it can pilfer from the world engine or if humans are wasting a precious resource, one better spent on healing the damage they have caused while eking out an existence they so arrogantly assume its people are entitled to.

Most humans have no clue about the price some have paid for their existence and that of their scions. It is for those who have sacrificed, and those who still do, that deserve Life's colorful charade, an aspect other humans have so carelessly wasted by engaging in actions unbecoming of the spirit of conception.

As humans stare into the dark abyss of their minds, searching for more, is it blind Hope that something will answer them, or is it the resonating Fear that nothing will keep humanity frozen like frightened children? Does humanity wonder if the Eide they seek may be a tempest beyond perception, a distillation of their creation, or just maybe a wild thing best left to roam the hollow dungeons of their mind and to its own devices?

Furthermore, should humans be attempting to invoke that which wove them from the stars? Is humanity truly prepared to test its resolve, its meager existence, upon the anvil of creation? If so, consider this: What do humans desire out of Life? Could it be to know who they are? Where do they come from? Why were they made? What is in store for them? When will it come to pass? How can humanity become more? If this is the case, to whom should humans pose these questions?

These relative queries are the cogs that drive humanity. However, the passion for acquiring such knowledge brings with it a disturbance of comprehension. Through such measures, humans learn that Eternity exists, not in perpetuity for them or anything they will ever know. (This is reflective of what Hector Berlioz said: "Time is a great teacher, but unfortunately it kills all its pupils.") The end of existence is a troublesome dilemma for some but an intriguing concept for others. The confusing aspect for most is that the end exists for no purpose but to detract from the world and dismantle its creation.

The interesting concept referenced above is that taking ownership reveals how temporal everything in Life is, and that we should make the best of what humanity has been given, rather than squander it. Both methods have their merits, but in the end, what gives society the right to question such an existence or even attempt to tamper with the order of Life's design?

Is it humanity's self-induced delusions of Godhood prompting them to meddle with the threads of creation's tapestry? If so, then who is there to keep them in check so they do not upset the delicate balance of its cosmic paragon? If not, why do humans spend so much Time and effort on something they cannot affect? Such an action would be a moot point in the grand scheme of things, as Life purposes as it wills. This author would surmise that such questions fall within the realm of ego and the boundaries of decency.

The sentient mind is resolutely infatuated with Life, and it exists for more than being born to die. It cannot fathom such a waste of creation's will. To try to separate Life into pieces or to fathom the surface static of its design parameters would be ego at its most trying. Humanity lacks the knowledge, brainpower, or conceptual framework to comprehend such an enigmatic truth.

It is truly beyond understanding. Humans can hypothesize all they want, but this is all it will ever be. (Roger Penrose wrote, "Consciousness ... is the phenomenon whereby the universe's very existence is made known.") Humans are masters of their own lives - up to a point - and as such, it has been suggested to them to engage in such activities for reasons that are not fully understood. They control its quiddity, longevity, and continuation ... for a Time.

Humans are all pieces of Life's miraculous existence, of its penultimate architect(s). We are, in the author's belief, all fragments taken from this essence to experience every single physical Choice possible. Until every route is explored, humans cannot return to the cradle of their origin and reconstitute their creator's natural form. (The Big Bang theory would lend credibility to this ideation, particularly if one considers the prospect of the creator's essence being that which was strewn out across the universe.)

Ponder this: What if, at some point in Life, there arose an opportunity that allowed humans to question their maker(s)? Have any of us contemplated the questions we might pose and the relative answers we Hope to receive?

In this position, would anyone want to know the truth, especially if it somehow damaged them? Has anyone considered what they would do upon receiving the answers they are seeking? What then? How would each person respond to such answers? Would they then take what was passed on to them and weave it into something that promotes progression, or manipulate what was given into something crafted for Deceit? Would each answer be a blessing or a curse? Would it be more than just a desire to satisfy idle curiosity or to drum up more questions that require further explanation, akin to a child asking the irritating, repetitive questions of "Because why?" and "How come?"

Consider the intent of the following quotes: "Some questions don't have answers, which is a difficult lesson to learn." – (Katherine Graham), and, "It is better to ask some of the questions than to know all the answers." – (James Thurber).

With that being said, how would humans feel about their maker(s) after receiving such answers, or if they were not proffered any response at all? Would they walk away from their creator(s) with feelings of understanding, confusion, fulfillment, emptiness, pride, shame, happiness, anger, satisfaction, disgust, peace, fury, or just plain carelessness and contempt?

Would one of the first questions asked be, "Why am I here?" If so, what if the answer proffered diminished one's desire to live? What if it banished any thoughts of a self-assumed right to exist? What if the answer was, "You were an experiment," or " It was for sport?" "For food." Could one handle such a cold shot of reality to the face? What if humans did not receive an answer at all? Would one assume they have a right to one or even be bold enough to demand one? What if the answers were incomprehensible to their mind? What would one think then?

However, pause for a moment to ponder if humans have considered what questions might be asked of them. What might the creator(s) think of humanity, of how they would attempt to explain each action taken in Life, their mistakes, their careless nature? How would humans feel if the creator(s) could not spare even a second for their creations? Would humans think their creator(s) owe them as much? Would humans tell them off like anyone else who offended them, with angry contempt and indignation?

In reality, the Fear of what humans might conjure from the unknown or impose upon themselves should be the trammels that guard humanity's fragile nature against its pregnant vanity. This search for meaning and clarity will be the bane of its existence, especially when assuming one can reason with their own 'Unreasonable Insanity.' -

[Okay, back to the primary subject matter]

The foundation of Faith is a complex idea for most people, yet it is a simple undertaking anyone can embrace. It is open to each person's interpretive relation and how they wish to cultivate it for their own Life. The only exception to this rule is when one's Faith promotes servitude rather than the freedom to practice or engage in what pleases them. Such a measure of conformity does not foster freedom of Faith but rather a form of dictatorial submission, which no Faith should endorse. When genuine, Faith is meant to inspire and benefit the practitioner, not impose servitude.

Regardless of how each person perceives Faith, it is a complex engagement that can lead to suffering, disappointment, failure, and Deceit. Yet, others argue that it is practical, as it can instill confidence, ambition, Courage, and Hope in those in need of such a blessing. Faith can be whatever one wishes, as it is a creation of the mind, a measure of strength in one's moment(s) of most actual need, and in those instances where others could benefit from its boon. It may indeed cause injury, heartache, and even Death, but it also compels humanity to set one foot in front of the other and continue to push itself beyond the Fears troubling the Life it chooses to live.

The notion of Faith is a unique indulgence, an endless yearning for something more. It is a concept one places confidence in, a commitment of trust and Loyalty to that which can help elevate the mind and spirit, thereby breaking the bonds of restrictive consciousness they are bound by, meaning those infused into our society. It is not a manifestation of Fear but a by-product of Despair and uncertainty. This method of conscious engagement likely stemmed from a dire need or longing for something missing in their Lives, most likely shaped by a mind consumed by desperation or by a notion designed as a protective measure to combat the harsh reality of their inherent loneliness. This reminds me of a relative quote by Richard Wright. It reads, "Man can starve from a lack of self-realization as much as they can from a lack of bread."

As I mentioned earlier, Faith can be a crutch for some people to lean on in Times of need. It can also be tapped to inspire raw creativity and instill Courage in those who Fear change and the unknown. It can also breed confidence in those lacking self-belief and create a strong bond that not even a person's worst Fears could fracture. H.L. Mencken said, "Faith may be defined briefly as an illogical belief in the occurrence of the impossible." In some ways, I believe in the impossible, as long as it is not beyond the ability to create or accomplish. Things beyond such measures are improbable and should never be considered in the same context.

Faith is one of the most profound expressions of humanity's existence. If one has managed to fortify the Faith in one's Life and has woven its essence around one's being to the point of absolutism, no aspect of human nature can trump it. The mental fortitude it promotes in the mind's eye is so narcotizing that such practitioners have been known to pressure themselves to engage in matters they would typically shy away from without the dire need for self-preservation. This summons a quote by Edmund Burke: "All men that are ruined, are ruined on the side of their (own) natural propensities."

Faith can also be utilized to create Fear and Doubt, demons of one's own making, which is what propaganda instills. Such an essence can be used to subdue others to the point that their minds are influenced, allowing others to prey upon the Fears hidden among the prayers of the hopeful. One must be cautious as to the methods of Faith, as no one is exempt from such measures, especially any unsuspecting party. This reminds me of a sentiment I crafted about Faith several years back; it reads, "Faith is the deceiver of self-reliance. It is a blinding shroud to mask our reality and a morbid crutch to comfort a lack of resolve." – T.C. Monk

Humans have an extraordinary knack for believing anything they set their minds to, regardless of how strange and outlandish it might seem to anyone else. Nothing is beyond the scope of thought, especially when creating a place where one feels wanted or accepted by one's class. The more one tells/convinces oneself that something is true, the more the mind will find a way to take and assume that reality. There is a niche for everyone in the world, regardless of one's beliefs or interests. There are no limits but those we set for ourselves. To paraphrase Eric Hoffer, "Faith in a cause is to a relative degree a poor substitute for the lost trust in ourselves."

For the many reasons stated herein, the Eide of Faith, having been cultivated by humanity, is a measure that truly belongs in its current state. It is not an object or affair that wove itself from nothing, but an essential part of our symbiotic and parasitic existence. There is a reason for its presence, a substance of sentient value one cannot truly grasp. One can hypothesize all they want, but no one knows for sure why. The most recognizable theme is that it was created to counter the self-doubt and uncertainty that humans constantly fill their minds with.

However, what is strange is that, despite most of humanity understanding the concept of Faith as the eternal search for truth—a thing they will never see—they still tend to thrive on what they Hope exists. And despite their best efforts to Will it into existence, they have yet to figure out how to use it properly to stabilize their strangled, imperfectly balanced lives. It is an enigma, but an affair one can only Hope humanity someday finds a solution to without destroying who and what they are. To allow it to consume one wholly defeats the purpose of fighting for a belief or a cause of one's own in the first place.

Allow me to elaborate further. When Faith becomes predominant in someone to the point of utter devotion or personal failure, it can compel them to offer up their very being to preserve its core belief. And, that by and through such an extreme act of self-betrayal for such an ideal can ultimately instill a powerful conviction in others, one that will drive them to either match or surpass what they have witnessed or heard, as it relates to any such acts of Faith-based oblation. This conduct will manifest itself into a sense of unparalleled ruin that will convince the believer (with absolute certitude) that their Life has always been destined to be sacrificed for this cause alone. Such are the brainwashing techniques used to control the subordinate masses, once the teachers of its ideology do not actively or willingly participate in it unless it is by force!

Here, I'd first like to include a piece written by Bertrand Russell, along with a further description of Faith (Wikipedia):

- Christians hold that their Faith does good, but other faiths do harm. At any rate, they hold this about the communist Faith. What I wish to maintain is that all faiths harm. We may define "Faith" as a firm belief in something for which there is no evidence. Where there is evidence, no one speaks of "Faith." We do not speak of Faith that two and two are four or that the earth is round. We only speak of Faith when we wish to substitute emotion for evidence. This substitution of emotion for evidence is apt to lead to strife since different groups substitute different emotions.' "Christians have Faith in the Resurrection; communists have Faith in Marx's Theory of Value. Neither Faith can be defended rationally, and each is defended by propaganda and, if necessary, by war." – (Bertrand Russell)

Faith and rationality are two ideologies that exist in varying degrees of conflict or compatibility. Rationality is based on reason or facts. Faith is belief in inspiration, revelation, or authority. "Faith" sometimes refers to a belief held without reason or evidence, a belief held despite or against reason or evidence, or a belief based upon a degree of evidential warrant.

Although the words "Faith" and "Belief" are sometimes erroneously conflated and used as synonyms, Faith properly refers to a particular type (or subset) of beliefs, as defined above.

Broadly speaking, there are two categories of views regarding the relationship between Faith and rationality:

1) Rationalism asserts that truth should be established through reason and factual analysis rather than Faith, dogma, tradition, or religious teaching.

2) Fideism asserts that Faith is essential and that beliefs can be held without any evidence or reason, even contradicting evidence and reason.

The Catholic Church also taught that true Faith and correct reason can and must work together and, appropriately viewed, can never conflict, as both have their origin in God, as stated in the Papal encyclical letter issued by Pope John Paul II, Fides et Ratio ("[On] Faith and Reason")

- Relationship between Faith and Reason -

The relationship between Faith and reason has been a topic of hot debate since the days of the Greek philosophers. Plato argued that knowledge is simply the memory of the eternal. Aristotle established principles by which knowledge could be discovered through reason.

Rationalists point out that many people hold irrational beliefs for many reasons. There may be evolutionary causes for irrational beliefs; irrational beliefs may increase our chances of survival and reproduction. Or, according to Pascal's Wager, it may be to our advantage to have Faith because Faith may promise infinite rewards, while the rewards of reason are seen by many as finite. Another reason for irrational beliefs may be explained by operant conditioning, as seen in a study by B.F. Skinner. In 1948, Skinner's pigeons were rewarded with grain at regular intervals, regardless of their behavior. The result was that each pigeon developed an idiosyncratic response, which became associated with the consequences of receiving grain. [1]

Believers in Faith—for example, those who believe salvation is possible through Faith alone—frequently suggest that everyone holds beliefs arrived at by Faith, not reason. [2] We believe that the universe is a sensible place and that our minds, through Faith, allow us to arrive at correct conclusions. Rationalists contend that this conclusion is reached because they have observed the world to be consistent and sensible, not because they have Faith that it is.

- Beliefs held "by Faith" may be seen existing in several relationships to rationality -

Faith as underlying rationality:

In this view, all human knowledge and reason depend on Faith: Faith in our senses, Faith in our reason, Faith in our memories, and Faith in the accounts of events we receive from others. Accordingly, Faith is seen as essential to and inseparable from rationality. According to René Descartes, rationality is built on the realization of the absolute truth, "I think, therefore I am," which requires no Faith. All other rationalizations are built outward from these realizations and are subject to falsification at any Time with the arrival of new evidence. (Cf. - scientific theory changes in much the same manner.) [Cf. emphasis added.]

Faith as addressing issues beyond the scope of rationality:

In this view, Faith addresses issues that science and rationality are inherently incapable of addressing, yet are nevertheless entirely accurate. Accordingly, Faith complements rationality by answering questions that would otherwise be unanswerable.

Faith as contradicting rationality:

In this view, Faith is seen as holding views despite evidence and reason to the contrary. Accordingly, Faith is seen as pernicious with respect to rationality, as it interferes with our ability to think, and, conversely, rationality is seen as the enemy of Faith, as it interferes with our beliefs.

Faith and reason are essential together:

This is the Catholic view that Faith without reason leads to superstition, while reason without Faith leads to nihilism and relativism.

Faith as based on warrant:

In this view, some degree of evidence provides a warrant for Faith. "To explain great things by small."

In conclusion, what should boggle one's mind about Faith is how all the people on this planet happen to engage in the same type of manifestation of the mind, even though they have never met before. Could it be some shared mental state that somehow connects all human beings in a more existential sense? Or, might it be a sense that humans share more subconsciously, a means of comfort and inspiration, one that compels them to seek out what makes them feel more robust, more in control, and not lost in the streams of passing Time? If so, it will also weaken them, making them more susceptible to 'The Ties That Bind' and its desire for connectivity and belonging, uniting all of humanity.

– DOUBT –

(17)

The word "Doubt" is a noun. It is described as an uncertainty about something, an undecided state of mind, a tendency to Doubt, or a lack of concrete proof. It also means feeling unsure about something, hesitating to believe, trust, or question.

* * *

Doubt has been a big part of my Life since my youth, and at one point in Time, I doubted everything I believed, especially the forced indoctrination of society and its relative conformity. I thought, 'Why must I believe what someone else tells me?' 'Why am I not permitted to believe how I choose?' These thoughts stemmed not only from the many things in my Life that didn't make sense, but also from the lack of quality answers to explain their assorted mysteries. It was not until much later in Life that I learned that not every question has an answer, especially those queries that cannot be proven beyond a reasonable Doubt.

Most people do not understand the vital importance of Doubt and how deeply it can negatively affect a person's Life. This five-letter word (Doubt) is a straight razor that cuts deep into humanity's cycle of existence and can be the Death dealer of self-reliance. This notion not only has the propensity to fill the mind with hesitation and uncertainty, but it can also generate one's worst Fears, even if they are entirely baseless. Many relationships (friends, family, lovers, and work) have ended in disaster because of this concept, most of which were likely ruined based on the threads of one's own making.

This author does not believe there is a cure for such an affliction, regardless of it being something intangible and only existing in one's head. Its effects are no less potent simply because it is a contrivance of the mind. The more one feeds and nurtures their non-physical nature, the more it will thrive and become virulent, eventually consuming them like a malignant parasite. Why it affects humanity as it does is a bit of a mystery, but such is the nature of the beast, comparable to the allegory of the frog and the scorpion.

The pressures of Doubt are an eldritch occurrence in humanity's overall existence. No one is exempt from its influence, as it pervades everything and everywhere. It is a product that seeps into humans' minds like a malevolent voice spreading its sermon. Its essence will attempt to convince them they are in danger from something unknown to them, a thing beyond their ability to perceive, control, affect, or escape from. How strange it is that humans can create their own worst Nightmares out of nothing, fueled by a sense of pure paranoia, and convince themselves that danger and Death lurk around every corner, even though they may not.

Furthermore, this touch of madness will affect all of humanity, at one Time or another, throughout their lives. Doubt is not an affair anyone can step away from as though it does not exist, nor should they attempt to dismiss it as nonsense. There is one reason it is Present in our world, even if it is initially veiled. Perhaps it is there to give us pause, a moment to consider the uncertain, the unknown, or all the angles of what we wish to engage in before advancing. Perhaps it serves as a measure for humans to assess whether something is worth the risk of investigation, or to give us Time to prepare for the unknown Future That may unfold with its advent.

The quiddity of Doubt centers on uncertainty and reservation and can instill deep skepticism in those unfortunate enough to experience it. The product it conjures can not only cause one to betray their confidence in any engagement with Life, but, if left unchecked, also breed Fear in myriad ways and places. This reminds me of what Bertrand Russell said about Doubt: "The trouble with the world is that the stupid are cocksure, and the intelligent are full of Doubt." Additionally, Aldous Huxley intimated regarding skepticism, "I am too much of a skeptic to deny the possibility of anything."

Doubt is 'resistance' in its purest measure, a subject Steven Pressfield wrote about in his book, 'The War of Art.' I agree that resistance is humanity's Achilles' heel, but it can also be its greatest asset. At its core, it is a contradictory essence, an aspect humans must engage in to conquer their nature. One moment may cause an individual to remain in their comfort zone and avoid the unknown. While another moment will prod them to chance the uncertain to reveal the unknown, which is a manifestation of progression in its penultimate form: "To philosophize is to Doubt." – (Montaigne).

If humanity fails to heed its senses and feelings of Doubt, it will simply be gambling with everything it is to test its mettle against the fortifications of Life. But for what reason? Is it to demonstrate something to others or verify something to themselves? Could it be to prove that Doubt is not their master? Or is it to assume a certain amount of risk out of a sheer sense of bravado? No one truly knows the answer to such questions, as each person's quality of Doubt varies, as does their desire for risk versus reward. Everything humans engage in is calculated in this manner. It differs only in degree, depending on whether they are for or against it, based on their participation in each measure at the Time.

In any real sense, Doubt can be viewed as a cognitive condition in which the mind is nant between a collection of disputed proposals and incapable of acceding to any particular position, especially if it can prompt one to suspend or decline any such Future engagements. One's level of Doubt is indeed fostered by emotional decisions, a conceptual design nestled between confidence and dubiety. This ideation may include concepts such as skepticism, disbelief, a lack of belief in any situation, modus operandi, assumed truth, purpose, or a quantifiable position.

- Doubt is a mental state in which the mind remains suspended between two or more contradictory propositions, unable to assent to any of them. Doubt, on an emotional level, is a state of indecision between holding and not holding a belief. It may involve uncertainty, distrust, or lack of conviction on specific facts, actions, motives, or decisions. Doubt can delay or prevent relevant action due to concerns about mistakes or missed opportunities.

In premodern theology, Doubt was "the voice of an uncertain conscience" and essential to realize because when in Doubt, "the safer way is not to act at all."

Doubt sometimes calls on reason. Doubt may encourage people to hesitate before acting and/or to apply more rigorous methods. Doubt may be significant as it leads to disbelief or non-acceptance. When it comes to politics, ethics, law, or any decisions that often determine the course of an individual's Life, most people tend to place great importance on Doubt and to foster elaborate adversarial processes to sort through all available evidence carefully.

Societally, Doubt creates an atmosphere of distrust. It is accusatory and de facto alleges either foolishness or deceit on the part of another. Western European society has fostered a stance that opposes tradition and authority since the Enlightenment.

Sigmund Freud's psychoanalytic theory attributes Doubt (which may be interpreted as a symptom of a phobia originating in the ego) to childhood, when the ego develops. These theories maintain that childhood experiences can instill Doubt about one's abilities and even one's very identity.

Cognitive, mental, and spiritual approaches abound in response to the wide variety of potential causes for Doubt. Behavior therapy, in which a person systematically asks his mind whether the Doubt has any factual basis, uses rational, Socratic methods. This method contrasts with the Buddhist Faith, which involves a more esoteric approach to Doubt and inaction. Buddhism views Doubt as a negative attachment to one's perceived Past and Future. Letting go of one's personal history (affirming this release every day in meditation) plays a central role in releasing the doubts that have developed within it and become attached to it.

Partial or intermittent negative reinforcement can create an effective climate of Fear and Doubt. [2]

Descartes employed the Cartesian Method of Doubt as a preeminent methodological approach in his foundational philosophical investigations. Branches of philosophy, like logic, devote much effort to distinguishing the dubious, the probable, and the certain. Much illogic rests on dubious assumptions, data, or conclusions, with rhetoric, whitewashing, and deception playing their accustomed roles. – (Wikipedia)

In summation, it would be prudent if humanity took the Time to recognize that "Uncertainty dines on hesitation. Hesitation feeds off resistance. Resistance promotes one's measure of anticipatory concern, which by proxy, breeds the myriad reasons of Doubt that manifest within us all." – T.C. Monk

– COURAGE –

(18)

The word "Courage" is a noun. It is defined as having the ability to disregard one's Fears, to have bravery, or to be brave. It is also the lack of Fear or apprehension in the face of danger or adversity.

* * *

As I grew older, I learned to appreciate Courage for what it is and what it can offer to those in need. While I contemplated the depth of this unique protagonist, I became aware of the multifaceted thespian within and how it can help others cast off the shroud of solace and complacency. Such an aspect can serve as a shield or barrier against the negative influences that bombard us daily. It has no master, no nemesis, and cannot be corrupted. One of the most beneficial aspects we can glean from Courage is its ability to combat the pressures of Fear, Doubt, and Despair. And, if we are mindful, we might be capable of altering the product of these afflictions and strategically shaping the seeds of confidence, fortitude, and resolve from their ashes.

When considering the profile of Courage, one must recognize that logic and reason constantly oppose humanity's desire to venture into the unknown. This opposition creates a dichotomy in the decisions one makes. However, Courage impels one to continually move forward in pursuit of the undiscovered and daringly trespass into the domain of the unfamiliar.

There is no legitimate reason to proscribe everything that might pose a risk. The only reason one might do so is that they think or assume they might lose something if something goes awry. However, this is a presupposition on their part, and it is the crux of such reasoning. There is nothing in Life one could potentially lose if one chooses to take the uncertain chance. There is not a single thing in Life that genuinely exists as a quantifiable object of actual worth. The only matters with estimable merit are those that humans give a qualitative value to, such as one's Life, possessions, or any aspect of need and want. How humans estimate the worth of a particular thing, generally speaking, is based on its relative importance to each person. It is called 'desire,' which is reflected in one's need or want ... except for sustenance and air.

Courage requires strong consideration and conviction to be worth something (to someone), yet this is also confined within the user's pragmatic essentialist boundaries. Courage is not so much a physical confinement or reality as some people like to assume, but rather a mental stimulant and captivation of the instant, an essence feeding on one's covetous nature and the desire to challenge one's place in the pecking order of Life.

There is no other reason to test one's fortitude than to see where—exactly—one belongs in the food chain. However, if one genuinely desires to know this, Life will undoubtedly put them in their place if they dare to test those boundaries. Mother Nature is patient and understanding, but she is also the consummate parent when she needs to school her progeny and set them to task.

Most people are content with remaining on the same rung of comfort as almost everyone else, but then some cannot, or will not, be sustained by mere apathy. These types of people need struggles in Life, strife, conflict, and progression. They must challenge the cosmos for their right to assume the next rung on the ladder of ascension. Remaining idle (stagnant) is not a path to advancement, as it wastes valuable Time and energy.

Elevation is significant to certain people's mental health, ego, and quality of Life. Some would say it is more intricate than this, more complex, but it is not. It is intrinsic and draws its compulsion from the mind, which shapes who and what humans are and determines the innate qualities that govern their predilections. Overall, Courage is a way for humanity to test its worth, build mental fortitude, build status, challenge its place in creation—to stand out—and evolve in an ever-changing world.

It takes a constant effort to contact or remain connected to the Courage within. This endeavor will enable individuals to overcome the resolute self-preservation that undoubtedly afflicts everyone. This will become crucial to humanity's existence and progress, particularly when it involves any engagement with risk.

The first moment one feels the essence of Courage come over them, they will never forget that strange and exhilarating sensation. It will completely overwhelm them, much like a synthetic stimulant promoting a sense of invincibility, one which can cause them to disregard any fundamental understanding of the danger they might be exposing themselves to without even knowing it. Approaching anything with foolhardiness gives others the impression that one's Life is inconsequential or that they are indifferent to success in their endeavors. This behavior indicates a lack of respect for Life and a willingness to sacrifice anything or anyone without a second thought.

Courage takes Time to come to fruition, but when it does, it will provide one with a clear understanding that whatever they are willing to fight for or sacrifice must be worth the price exacted.

It does not mean diving headlong into anything with reckless abandon, but approaching it with apprehension and speculative concern. However, if one fails to do so, it may not bode well for those around them, as it might force others to sacrifice for something they may not have been willing to do under different circumstances. This is reminiscent of what G.B. Shaw wrote: "Self-sacrifice enables us to sacrifice other people without blushing."

As I mentioned earlier, "Once a person experiences Courage for the first Time ...," they will have a clear baseline for how it generally affects them. They can then take the Time to review and assess the entire experience and make the necessary adjustments. It is not a difficult concept to grasp; it simply requires dedication and discipline to act appropriately. One must desire this outcome for oneself. Otherwise, it will fail on its own merits before it becomes a reality.

Over Time, the Courage one eventually gains will become infused with a sense of responsibility and self-control. This will enable them to master their emotions and remain calm and collected during Times of panic and stress. It will also allow one to take control of one's surroundings and improve one's chances of making rational decisions that would otherwise be left to chance, leading to uncertain consequences.

However, do not mistake Courage for lack of caution or plain recklessness, as both concepts have their place in reality. For clarity, the following quotes should provide a vivid picture of how versatile the concept of Courage truly is and how its engagement is so mercurial and mutable that, according to Virgil, "... it is fickle and changeable like a woman."

In keeping with this theme, please take a moment to consider how the following quotes reflect this subject and circumscribe it in a finite sense.

"Courage mounteth with occasion." – (Shakespeare)

"Until the day of his Death, no man can be sure of his Courage." – (Jean Anouilh)

"Heroing is one of the shortest living professions." – (Will Rogers)

"Courage is the absence of apprehension and the foundation of one's true mettle." – T.C. Monk

"Fortune sides with him who dares." – (Virgil)

- Shakespeare's quote, "... occasion," implies it is a matter of circumstance. Virgil's quote "dares" implies that one be bold or chance the unknown. The remaining quotes are self-explanatory. -

No person can be certain of their reaction to any situation, as each is unique and cannot be planned in advance. This is magnified exponentially when one is forced to face such critical decisions. This principle also applies to instances where individuals create fictional scenarios to test their reactions, an exercise used to puzzle out what their reaction should be, even though none of it is fact-based science.

Fight, flight, and freeze are all kinesthetic reactions to situations one might encounter. These particular modes of engagement will require an extensive, immediate evaluation of each predicament. Each reflex will need a specific response based on the severity of the threat. No two scenarios will ever be alike, nor will they feel related. So, any preplanned reactionary measures one might conceive of will never play out in the manner they were designed to, as the variations would be too numerous to cover and spoil one's Choice.

Courage is a dual factor in one's Life. It carries a relatively simple description yet holds significant weight in its overall quality and set curve. It is not something every person possesses, but it is a trait every human should strive to attain. To seek and follow such a path is no easy decision. It takes grit, perseverance, and fortitude to follow through on this. It will test one's strength of mind, character, heart, ambition, and resolve.

Despite how one wishes to script its raw quiddity, its base essence will not change. The crucible of circumstance forges its structure, and it is the one character trait that humans can possess, which will never stop testing their steadfastness. It is doubtful there is anything in Life that is as relentless as the attire of fortitude. It is not a suit that just anyone can wear well. It takes true backbone not only to sport an ensemble such as this but also to be worthy of what it can bestow upon its wielder.

Unfortunately, many people who try to incorporate Courage into their wardrobe often assume they can wear it and take it off like a comfortable pair of shoes, especially when it suits them. To truly understand this trait, one must recognize their willingness to take on particular challenges, acknowledge their limitations, and understand that without risk, there can be no reward.

– FEAR –

(19)

The word "Fear" is a noun. It is defined as feeling panic or distress brought on by exposure to danger, the expectation of pain, uncertainty, or loss.

***

The current school of thought regarding Fear is that it is solely a product of human design, resulting from uncertain cause-and-effect relationships and shaped by both objective pressures and subjective influences. I agree with this base assumption, but there is more to Fear than this. I would include the fact that it can also be an aspect of self-contrived paranoia. An essence such as this is a troublesome annoyance in Life, an element most people struggle with. Its wearisome draw can grind on a person's sanity, almost to the point of depleting their will to sustain.

However, in the real world, there are mortal things one should have a healthy respect for, especially if one wishes to survive any unfortunate encounters. The real questions one should be pondering are:

1) Can an aspect of internal apprehension exist without visual acquisition?

2) Will it manifest without a threat-level event?

3) Are such things conjured by one's personal experience?

The answer to these three queries is yes. In some instances, it can be, much like phobias, because Fear of the unknown allows such things to occupy one's thoughts.

Those who say, "The things humans Fear are merely products of their invention," surely do not understand the nature of its essence. If this were the case, how can one Fear a thing without knowing or comprehending the danger it may or may not pose? They cannot! Again, this is comparable to what a phobia does. The simple truth is that Fear works in mysterious ways, and each person forms their own concept based on what they see, feel, hear, and sense (the latter being anything not entirely factual). Some might pause at the last reference and ask why anyone would need to process any aspect that is not fact-based. This is more prudent when one realizes that so much depends on one's perspective and perception.

It is strange to consider something a threat to one's Life or safety, especially if it may not have been a thing to Fear in the first place. I am confident that such a response is due to how a thing is presented to a person, or to how humans create their own comprehensive and reactive relation to it. This is where science fails to provide a definitive answer, leaving one to ponder whether what they sense is real or an illusory construct of the mind, for reasons unknown.

Humanity needs its Fears, regardless of whether they are self-induced or influenced by external forces. Such measures are the only things that offer one a brief pause, a moment to consider what they choose to indulge in, especially if it may endanger their current Life design. Fear should be a marker in one's Life, not a terminal point that defines one's relative existence. It should be used as an equalizer, particularly when humans decide to pit their chances of success against the level of assumed risk in all they do.

Everything humans experience in Life, whether personally or through others, can create a sense of Fear in them. The strength of such a manifestation can be determined by how much Time one allocates to evaluate its true nature. Humans should learn to respect their Fears rather than dread, fight, or be consumed by them. Without the trammels of Fear, the world would be a much different place, more chaotic and damaging to the senses than ever imagined. Albeit, a healthy dose of Fear is a measure of comfortable restriction in Life. Such an aspect could be likened to a yellow caution light on a street post, serving not only to temper the mind's indulgences but also to protect what nature has given to Life.

Furthermore, the longer humanity contemplates the possibilities of what may occur if they employ such measures, the more Fear one can have in the mind. Some people devote their entire lives to figuring out how to corrupt, abuse, or master it, and when humans think this way, they tend to create unease within themselves. This anxiety comes from the thoughts of, "What if it does not go my way?" " What if something goes wrong?" or "What if something happens to me?" This concept is known as 'Anticipatory Concern,' the true nature of how all Fears are created.

As intimated in an earlier section, Fear touches every human being in one form or another, but how one reacts to it depends on how one consumes it. This is in conjunction with the 'fight, flight, or freeze syndrome' referenced in the Courage section of this work, all of which are conditions based on Fear. These traits have their own applications for each person and the ways they will condition their victims.

Inductive and deductive reasoning do not conform to a particular set of parameters regarding Fear, yet draw their baseline from the physical laws of empirical knowledge. It would be nice if pragmatism were the only adequate resource one drew from, but such is not the case with Fear. This beast of burden has its own methods for weaving its suggestive nature into the receptive minds. Learning precisely where humanity's Fears stem from and why they exist might be essential. Humans might be more at ease if they regard them as productive reasoning or a fabrication of necessity rather than a hindrance to growth, thereby preventing transcendence.

Regardless of how Fear is woven into the human collective, its infectious taint usually affects everyone similarly, though in varying degrees. This is a deceptive reality for some, as most of humanity thinks differently, even though many of the same things are involved. Now, this is not to say everyone reacts or responds the same way, but it does impact everyone regardless of race, creed, or gender. It is neither discriminatory nor selective in whom it chooses to sink its imaginary claws into, plaguing them with afflictions they can only imagine.

It may be crucial to designate Fear as a representative of overactive improvisation and speculative interpretation. It isn't easy to define all the parameters of this interpretive motif. Still, humanity must proactively approach this affliction, as it consumes a lion's portion of their lives. This type of corrective measure will help one manufacture a curative to restrain the creative hands of its relentless terrorism. Such an elective framework should enable one to take control of one's Fears or at least manage the allocation of anxiety to which one is subjected. This prohibitive action might allow humans to one day subdue their sensitivity to things they cannot control or perceive, whether in reality or in imagination.

Most people may never truly comprehend why Fear exists or that it may be Present to protect them from dangers they may not understand, especially the seemingly innocuous ones hidden beneath Life's deceptive facade. The strange thing about having Fears is that most humans allow them to be the controlling element in their lives and the governing factor in everything they do. I suggest that the amount one risks at any moment determines how much Fear rules their world.

With this in mind, I encourage everyone to harness their investigative abilities to be more mindful and less presumptive in the Future. Anyone can strive for self-improvement and personal growth by reflecting on their Fears and anxieties. Engaging with one's Fears through the lens of contemplative reasoning can be transformative. It offers an opportunity to gain a deeper understanding of ourselves and to overcome the Fears that hold us back.

– HONOR –

(20)

The word "Honor" is a noun. It is defined as having high respect or earning a quality reputation. It also speaks to the person's character upon which it is bestowed, that they strictly adhere to what is right, moral, ethical, and acceptable conduct.

* * *

There are many places in my Life where Honor has benefited me. Not only has it helped keep me beyond reproach, but it has also kept me out of the beast's jaws as well. However, when I first came across this term, before understanding it, I dismissed it as a tactic used by those who wish to portray themselves in a particular light. Notoriety is vital to some individuals, particularly those who require societal recognition. Whether this need comes from the individual or the collective does not matter. The only important aspect to them is how they wish to be perceived by others and the recognition and praise they can gain.

The naked truth about Honor is based on the common conscription and application of a moralistic code, one conjured and woven from the ideology of other people's quirks. Benevolence is a characteristic that can be attained through hard work, dedication, discipline, and determination. The problem is that rectitude and moral uprightness are not easy concepts for most people to uphold, as Honor causes one to struggle against the chains of freedom. This notion may be complex to grasp at first, but allow yourself (the reader) to think outside the box, as most of humanity has been trained to see things in a certain light and react in a particular manner.

Most people do not realize that Honor is not constructed from one's own standards but is shaped by societal preferences and norms of acceptability. Such control measures are introduced mainly by those who make the laws of the society one lives in and by those who lay the foundation of its ethos. Conformity is the main ingredient of Honor, and by that, society has been woven together. One can only assume that a concept such as this has been formulated to enhance the quality of Life among its adherents, provided they can adopt the essence of its precepts. It is something the individual will not only assume (depending on how it is presented to them) but also, if it appeals to their sense of custom, to the level of programming they have been subjected to, and to the image society has constructed of what it means to be honorable.

The structure of Honor is not only a quality meant to be held to the highest standard, but also to be adhered to in every aspect without fail. It is intended to be non-negotiable and not a fashionable prospect one should indulge in flippantly. It would undoubtedly take a person of strong constitution to adhere to these tenets, especially under extreme and challenging circumstances. However, its concept is not only a learned trait but is subjective and susceptible to outside influences. Some people will argue that its format is debatable regarding the nature of the relationship each attribute represents or what its characteristic should represent.

However, when it comes to Honor, nothing should be left to chance, as the path to its adoption is long and arduous. It will test one's resolve at every turn and measure every deed against the scales of altruism. By this standard, one succeeds or fails based on the actions one chooses.

This notion begins with understanding these precepts and their rationale, and then applying them to oneself. One must learn to be responsible for oneself before taking on responsibility for others or any other aspect of life. However, the dilemma hindering most people is their hidden dark side, a nature that can harm. Whether these types are born with such an affliction is unknown, but it is likely a learned trait or at least one influenced by an outside source.

Why this happens in this way is uncertain. However, it plays to a sense of laziness and a corrupt sense of being, which are assumed characteristics or habits. It may also stem from jealousy, a desire for what others have, and a longing for such things for oneself. Most of these types would rather take what others have than learn how to procure such materials for themselves. This brings to mind a quote I read long ago: "There is no such thing as right [or wrong] anyhow. It is a question of whether one can put it over. In any legal or practical sense, whatever is, is a right." – (Clarence Darrow)

Furthermore, throughout my Life, I have recognized that certain behaviors may be influenced by the solitude to which one is relegated. This position of isolation (or seclusion), whether forced by another or sought by one's own choice, remains an enigma. I would most certainly posit they are both coequal peddlers of violence and mischief. Such circumstances can manifest in ways that prevent one from recognizing the potential harm they may cause to others or to oneself.

That said, I assert that Honor is a Virtue earned, not given, and is available to everyone at any Time. It is neither discriminatory nor selective to those who wield its quality. And, even though it does not judge others as humans do, its distinction is gauged by each person. This assessment is determined by how it is viewed, as each person is affected by it and its impact on their environment. However, if one does not meet the strict criteria for its grace, it will be stripped of its honorary title until its actions are corrected, and it can one day reclaim its brand.

Honor is not a divisible trait in our society, but rather a preferable, favorable, and inviolable one. It creates a relatable, acceptable camaraderie among those cut from the same vine. In a society where this is a valuable and gradable concept, Honor is sacred to its class, not a variable tenet to its adherents.

As referenced earlier, no person can live by their scales, especially if they seek Honor or fame. These two aspects are measures sought when one chooses to mingle with, or be accepted by, society's social groups. However, suppose one decides to live a Life of solitude. In that case, one can set aside such conformity features and live unrestrained, provided one does not obstruct or inhibit anyone else from living as they choose.

However, the actions this solitary practitioner takes may ultimately leave them feeling more like a wild animal than a human being. Nature has its scales by which it will measure those who feed upon its essence, not just equally but savagely. The perfect quote for this aspect is one I penned years ago: "Honor is knowing what to do when to do it, and to practice temperance with every action." I also created an acronym for H.O.N.O.R., which stands for Handling One's Noble Oath Requirements.

The following is a compilation of ten precepts, one itemized in a manner that targets the natural principle of Honor according to most people in modern-day society:

1) Be courageous.

2) Be in harmony with nature.

3) Be of use, not a burden.

4) Seek peace, not war.

5) Protect the weak, the helpless, and the innocent.

6) Do not engage in ignoble acts.

7) Create Life and respect it.

8) Offer assistance to those in need.

9) Defend yourself and your family by any means.

10) Treat others as you would wish to be treated.

Regardless of which concept the quality of Honor holds for any person, the baseline principle must follow the conceptual nature by which the moral code was designed. This will allow all who partake in its desirable and beneficial properties to unequivocally reject any external influences that are unacceptable, unreasonable, and inconceivable to the heart of integrity and distinction.

– DISGRACE –

(21)

The word "Disgrace" is a noun. It is defined as an act or acts committed due to unfavorable or shameful conduct.

* * *

Before I learned what Life was about and how one should strive for progress, I set out on an unfettered trek through its chaotic menagerie without regard for anyone else. When I began this journey, I did not realize that each decision I made would have a significant impact on the years to come. I was too self-absorbed in doing things that pleased me, which brought me excitement, without a second thought about what I might be conjuring for myself down the road, how others viewed my actions, or how they might affect me.

I cannot explain (in any acceptable manner) why I chose to act in such a fashion when I was young, except to say I was utterly uninterested in anyone else's opinion of me. I wanted to do my own thing, and I took it as a challenge when others told me I could not. This became even more paramount when they told me there would be consequences for my actions, but again it instilled in me a sense of challenge: whether I could outdo them (and Life) at the game of chance. I did not realize at the Time that they (the adults) had been at this game far longer than I had, and far more experienced maneuvering through Life's curvature. I guess it was hubris on my part, thinking I was smarter than them because they were old and I was a foxy youngster. Oh, such is the ignorance of youth!

This fault in me was mainly due to my parents not being strict disciplinarians, which might have fostered hatred toward them, as I had experienced enough of that from my own parents. However, please do not assume I was never subjected to a belt or switch (at Times) for misbehaving; such is not an accurate measure of corrective discipline or an adequately structured learning method from which another human being (a child) can benefit. With enough Time, anyone can be beaten into submission. Still, such conduct is not an acceptable way to teach a child morals, respect, self-control, kindness, consideration, forgiveness, or the proper conduct for becoming a respectable adult. Such methods only instill Fear, disdain, and hatred in the heart of the abused.

However, when I was subjected to the belt or any other homegrown remedy meant for correction, I took it as a personal Wills test to see which one of us would break first, them ... or me. I was steadfast in my defiance and made it a point to show that I would not bow or acquiesce to violence against my person and that I would not submit to such barbaric tactics. I would say it became not only a matter of principle once I made up my mind to defy such objectionable treatment but a point of contention I would not be swayed from, regardless of what injury I might incur. This soon developed into a sense of how much I was willing to force myself to endure for such conviction, even if it was one born of ignorance and stubbornness. My Vice!

Due to this lack of correction, I had not learned what structure was, the proper discipline of the self, or what self-respect truly meant. It is strange to think now how much I wish I had acquired that in my Life, some measure that could have corrected my inability to listen, learn, and care for more than my feelings of comfort and contentment. This brings to mind a pertinent quote from Confucius about how those in power treat people. It reads: "If you control people by punishment, they will avoid crime but have no personal sense of shame. If you govern them using Virtue and control them with propriety, they will gain their sense of shame and thus correct themselves."

Confucius also taught that to be a better citizen or human being, one must look to oneself and comprehend that: 1) Learning without thought is labor lost. Thought without learning is perilous, 2) Real knowledge is knowing the extent of one's ignorance, and 3) when you see someone of worth, think how you may emulate them. When you see someone unworthy, examine your character. These are the things I wish I had learned when I was young, when I needed proper guidance and a solid mental framework.

It was not until later in Life - and before reading his teachings - that I came up with a concept somewhat mirroring what he intimated in section 3 above. It is strange to think my mind was on the same plane as his to come up with such a close comparison, which I have unfalteringly adopted in my Life since then. Its concept is, 'Whenever you meet someone, try to find some beneficial quality about them, a trait you favor or feel would benefit your Life, and adapt it to yourself. This can only make one a better person, not a worse one. If one engages in such an action long enough, the idea of the faultless self would manifest within and be prevalent and as close to perfection as one could achieve.' A perfect axiom if I have ever heard one!

Now that I am older, it is strange to realize how much of my thinking was based on defiance and pride, which stem from a misunderstanding of the true meaning and purpose of these ideas.

I can now say that I was in error in acting in such a manner in the places I did and against those individuals I levied them upon. However, is not Life a constant struggle to learn from our mistakes, one where our faults can teach us corrective measures if we understand why they mean something more than the words defining them? However, I cannot stifle the grating sound echoing in my head like trenchant laughter, especially when I think of the voices from the Past: "If I only knew then what I know now." "You will pay for this in the Future." – (Robert Wolff). If I had been exposed to these sentiments when I was young and understood their profound intent, it would have spared me a lot of pain and heartache, and it would not have taken as long to self-correct as it has.

Now, with that being said, I would ask one to consider why Disgrace would be an aspect any sane person would wish to employ. It is strange why anyone would seek this, but some individuals favor such a course of conduct as part of their hustle. The nature of such is enacted by those who have no Honor, no self-respect, nor a modicum of deference for others. These people have no regard for what others think, act, or feel at any given Time or place and assume they have carte blanche, regardless of the situation. Their primary concern is purely self-interest. They do not believe anyone else deserves what they do, nor should these people be treated any differently than they treat themselves.

Furthermore, in these types, their conduct is governed solely by a misguided sense of decency. Disgrace often stems from ignorance acquired from others, much as racism does. It can primarily arise from one of the following: being of a different gender, belonging to another culture, having an unusual physical appearance, holding an alternative belief system, having differences in knowledge, strength, or skill, or simply having a contrasting personality. There is no single reason for engaging in such behavior, but it often stems from one or more of these diversity-related conditions.

The following quotes should provide one with a moment of reflection concerning this:

"Oh, I have lost my reputation. I have lost the immortal part of myself, and what remains is bestial." – (Shakespeare)

"At every word [or deed], a reputation dies." – (Alexander Pope)

"I regard you with an indifference closely bordering on aversion." – (R.L. Stevenson)

The strength of such sentimentalism is pertinent in every way, but it is not a concept those who engage in Disgrace care about, as they follow R.L. Stevenson's maxim to the letter. Such thoughts go to what I once wrote:

"One has to respect another's opinion to care about what they think." – T.C. Monk

In addition, Disgrace is not only bound to how a person chooses to be, but it can also occur when one falls out of favor with other people. This can transpire through inappropriate actions or when one loses the respect or reputation they once enjoyed. When these things happen, it is usually because of something they have done themselves, not because anyone else has done something to them. Occasionally, it can happen by design of another, but it is ordinarily attributed to the former, not the latter.

When one falls out of favor with others, whether by their merit or another's, it does not mean they should be entirely written off, tagged as a pariah, and never be reassimilated again. However, suppose they seek this type of reacceptance or redemption. In that case, they will need to prove themselves seriously beyond a shadow of Doubt and reassure everyone affected by their actions that such acts will not recur. Second chances should be a thing one doles out like a rare bit of grace, but third chances should never happen, except where one has had false evidence manufactured against them.

When considering all aspects of this horrid beast called 'Disgrace,' it's essential to remember that most people may not live up to our ideals of honor or meet our expectations. When deciding how to interact with someone else and prevent such acts, one needs to be mindful of one's own conduct and preconceptions, as well as one's desire for a mutual connection with that person. Each of us has our own peculiarities and pet peeves, which may inadvertently hurt others. Such eccentricities provide us with variety in Life (like spice). They should be viewed this way, and not a stigmatizing occurrence to shun another because of, lest ye be shunned for a likewise right of indulgence.

– LOYALTY –

(22)

The word "Loyalty" is a noun. It is defined as a devotion or sentiment of attachment to a particular object, which may be a person, an ideal, a duty, or a cause. (For this section, I will not focus on political or religious fidelity but on its general form.)

* * *

I have given much thought to this concept and what it should contain. The sentiments I chose to infuse into it are my design and are meant to offer readers something to ponder. I believe that the interpretation of any aspect affecting our lives, to a certain degree, should be chock-full of poignant assertions capable of giving it a unique strength of its own. It should not be laced with one-sided opinions and subjective themes, especially those that could weaken its structural integrity and allow manipulation.

In creating this particular work, I needed to find a central path that would lead readers into a comfortable mindset, without making them feel overly put upon or dictated to. Such engagement methods weaken a person's message and minimize the educational quality of the overall piece. The idea is to show that everything readers find on the pages of this creation is meant to offer them a plethora of ideas to contemplate what this notion truly means to them and how they wish it to be an effective measure in their lives.

The interpretive motifs included in this work are not meant to be the sole facts that the readers should subscribe to when it comes to Loyalty. These illustrative examples are my musings on what this concept means to me and how I view it through the lens of my troubled Life. A subject such as this is not simple to define, nor should it be easy for any reader to consume. One should be compelled to consider the content of each page thoroughly and then carefully discern the collective verity that resonates with them the most. No two people's perspectives on this subject will be the same, nor should they be; however, the overall theme will remain cohesive within its general parameters. Therefore, I do not think there is a single correct way to view Loyalty in the perfect light, as it does not exist.

Most people are familiar with Loyalty, but few truly understand its scope. The principle behind this notion is neither difficult to grasp nor impossible to follow, as it is fundamentally conscious and conveys an essential quality that supports thought and action. An element like this not only requires shared trust among those with a common interest and like-minded goals, but also reflects the individual's interests and commitment to them.

Loyalty is an incredible test of Faith in oneself and those to whom it is proffered and received. Those who bestow Loyalty upon another tend to cede a measure of security and safety by surrendering their blind spot to that person, hoping they will protect it and not exploit it for their own gain. It will be the individual who either offers or receives it, creating an anomaly that cannot be accounted for and might pose a danger to them, particularly if they become a traitor-for-hire. Such an engagement is why I scripted the following quote: "Trust is a belief in fidelity and a razor that preys on stupidity." – T.C. Monk

Humans must come to grips with the fact that the more one gives to someone else, the less they have to count on themselves. In reality, Loyalty can be a strong ally or a deadly enemy, depending on how much trust one can allow it to consume them. Once a person incorporates this factor (trust) into the equation, they pollute their sense of security, forcing them to rely on others to determine when and where harm will come. It is a delicate balance, but a factor that must be tested at every turn, for one may never know when the hand of trust might strike them.

A measure of Loyalty exists for all things in Life. Yet, for humans, care must be taken regarding how it is actuated, as it can shift into zealotry when one loses one's sense of individuality and into resignation when exposed to reluctant acceptance. Unfortunately, Loyalty, in any respect, depends on how long its nature requires one's presence and how essential that presence is to the Future existence of its legacy. It is comforting to believe that someone will be loyal to another (or their cause), as they might claim, but most people fail to uphold this fundamental theme simply because they cannot be true to a factor that is inconsistent in one's Life.

To truly cement the Loyalty of another to oneself, or yours to them, depends on how indispensable one can make oneself. This means they must possess a unique quality or trait that the other person needs or cannot function without. The sole reason to make oneself invaluable, indispensable, and beyond compare is to stay the hand that threatens doom. This sentiment brings to mind the following two quotes by the same author: "Do unto others as you would that they would do unto you. Their tastes may be different," and "Take care to get what you like, or you will be forced to like what you get." – (G.B. Shaw).

One might ask if there truly is any absolute Loyalty in the world. My answer to this would be the same as was intimated in the previous sections: it would depend on the quality of the work and the extent to which they are needed. In a nutshell, if one can make oneself too valuable to lose, then yes! However, the strength of such fidelity should be constantly tested against the immediate needs. Take, for instance, Life. Is it loyal to itself? One may think this is a difficult question, but it is not. What if the same question were posed in a slightly alternate form: ' Will Life protect and nurture itself above all else?' The answer is, surprisingly, yes and no.

Now, one might ask how such is possible. Well, Life's Loyalty to anything is contingent on what it needs at the moment versus what it can do without, which is how one comes to understand the yes-and-no portion of the statement. For one to think Life is entirely loyal to any given thing is a ridiculous sentiment. The nature of sentient Life requires its creation(s) to strive for perfection and progression. This desire compels one to devise something more significant than what they were initially given. However, the problem with being devoted to such an endeavor is that the principle driving it (when need be) will always betray those of its order in the interest of securing its continued survival.

If progress becomes stultified in an unproductive manner, Life will terminate its design, with prejudice, in favor of another more proficient entity. Such a decisive measure defeats the Loyalty premise altogether, leaving one with an ill-favored feeling, which brings to mind a maxim I penned many years ago; it reads, "Loyalty is a specious calling. It breeds Death among its followers." – T.C. Monk

Furthermore, the same could be said for anyone in the world. Humans will be loyal to Life and unreliable, especially if one prioritizes the object at risk over one's own Life. For instance, if one has a spouse, a child, or a family member in grave peril, would they not - if Love is a factor - give their own Life to save them from harm, or worse? Of course, they would, unless they are selfish. The sacrifice of their existence would be the continuation of another's Life over their own!

Such contemplative motifs have become natural Life contingencies and are what the cycle of existence promotes. It chooses to fight for and save what it loves or needs by sacrificing what it can no longer use or what it deems less essential to its continued survival than what it is trying to protect. This has occurred throughout the world's history and in every aspect of creation. It is a recurring theme, known to some as 'Natural Selection,' but to most as the evolutionary process of Life. (N.B.: Some would argue that Loyalty is confined to the reciprocal type of personal interaction, not to that of inanimate objects. Such thoughts are subjective for some and a reality for others.)

This concept is quite limpid in the quotes I include here by the following three authors:

"Iron rusts from disuse, stagnant water loses its purity, and in cold weather, becomes frozen; even so, does inaction sap the vigors of the mind." – (Leonardo Da Vinci) [Swap 'mind' for 'Life']

"Every right implies a responsibility – every opportunity, an obligation – every possession, a duty." – (J.D. Rockefeller)

"Loyalty is an illusory notion, a prospect of mutual interest, one that is temporal at best." – T.C. Monk

– TREACHERY –

(23)

The word "Treachery" is a noun. It is a violation of one's trust, Faith, or word. It also means to betray the thing or person one is dealing with, or to deal with others dishonestly in a way that crosses one's sense of Virtue.

* * *

I am adding a short introduction here to highlight the diversity between Loyalty and Treachery, not only in how humans tend to misplace trust in one another, but also in how we often take one another's words or deeds for granted. It is not meant as an insinuation that all people are inherently untrustworthy, but rather to be conscious of the amount of Faith one places in others they do not know well. Tennessee Williams outlined this perfectly when he said, "We have to distrust each other. It's our only defense against betrayal."

Treachery is a dour and bothersome subject due to the belief and trust one places in those around them or in that which they Love. This type of naiveté undermines the fundamental rights of accountability and protection, both intended to be fostered through the mutual connections humans construct. Such notions are what people rely on to build beneficial, high-quality relationships that can last a lifetime. If this is not the reason humans do so, then what is the point of attempting to generate any connections with other people in the first place? It cannot be for selfish gain, as this would expose the disingenuous and deceitful side of every human being on the planet, thereby validating the theme of Treachery.

Imagine what it would be like if we all lived in a world where Treachery did not exist. It is a difficult concept for me to comprehend, mainly because I have lived with it for most of my Life and vaguely remember the quality I held in Loyalty as a child. It is strange to think how potent fidelity was to me at a young age, but not nearly as strong in its quality now that I am older. I genuinely miss the power it wove in my mind, whereby I could offer its quiddity to another and have them know it was beyond question. However, Time has tarnished its purity in my mind, making me almost entirely pessimistic about whom or what I can trust.

It is incredibly disconcerting how deeply this has affected me, especially when I know the Loyalty I have offered was without corruption. I wish I could proffer it to someone who would care for and protect not only its nature but the altruistic manner in which it was given. It's a lonely feeling to think I'm the only one who values Loyalty in this way. I know I am not the only one who still values it, but how can anyone be sure of another's conviction when all they have known for decades is Treachery? One can infer they believe they are giving or receiving 100%. Still, there will always be a bit of uncertainty in this, that small percentile that outweighs the more significant portion, which sows the seeds of Doubt in one's mind.

Be that as it may, I suggest that those who do not think this aspect concerns them look closely at what they assume is genuine in another person. This does not mean looking for ghosts in the basement, but rather being more cautious and attentive to their presumptions about one another. No one is beyond this measure of conduct unless they have never been exposed to it in their lifetime, which is hard to imagine today, even in the minutest fashion. But remember that if one goes looking for something of this caliber, they may not like what they find, as no one is perfect or without flaws.

For one not to realize that betrayal can occur at any moment is a form of ignorance in its purest sense. A person's Faith or trust in anyone else is conditional. It is quaint to think others will be unwavering in their resolve, but no one knows how another will react in any situation, especially if they do not understand what is at risk. Everyone has a price; anyone can be bought if—and only if—what is currently at stake is less valuable than what is presented to them. One must discover one's weaknesses, crutches, and sicknesses to exploit them. However, one must be willing to gamble with that subject's Fate and override one's sense of moral rectitude and strictures of conscience.

Such an engagement is not as easy to actuate as one might assume, as it is not a natural act but rather an unnatural deportment. It is a learned or practiced activity employed by either personal involvement, direct observation, or a measure of conceptual creation to advance the self. In their proximity to one another, humans are the enablers of such behavior, especially when one does not pay attention to what those around them are up to. A relationship, or friendship, must be constantly tested (at its edges) for signs of lack of integrity or commitment, lest one become a victim of its crumbling state of desuetude and "suffer the most unkindest cut of all." – (Shakespeare). Such connections are not weakened by disuse or complacency, but rather by the positive reinforcement each person infuses in them and by the challenges to their foundation.

The actions above resemble those of planet Life in that if they are starved for what they need to grow or sustain themselves, they will slowly wilt and die. It takes great care and patience to nurture such a thing and, in turn, measure blind Faith in another. However, there will be Times when it will fail, no matter how hard one tries or how much one feeds or supports such a relationship. It is not necessarily anyone's fault; rather, some things were not meant to be. No person can honestly know which ones are and which are not. It is a literal roll of the dice, a guessing game, a spin to chance the wheel of Fate.

In the author's opinion, these are matters that humanity should not only consider but also accept and address when evaluating the risks of eliciting Treachery from any interests they engage in. It is essentially a qualified acceptance: humans must acknowledge its existence and exercise great care not to promote it. Treachery is an evil seed that one should never tolerate in their Life. It is a measure born of hypocrisy and nourished by insecurity, greed, temptation, and one's careless nature. When one gives in to betrayal, they expose the baseness of their essence as an animal and their requisite desire to harm others, which is sadism in its most accurate form.

Furthermore, Treachery tends to be problematic for most people, as its very nature conjures up the most indelible and irksome pain, anger, Hate, regret, and violent tendencies dwelling in the hearts and minds of those it affects. It is an essence that tends to infuriate one beyond conscious concern for one's well-being. It also allows them to engage in Treachery themselves without considering the toll it will take on their core values. Strangely enough, when one participates in the betrayal of another, most subscribe to the following school of thought: "Do unto others before they do unto you, for you may never get the chance to strike back." – (Twist on the Golden Rule [Luke 6:31]) is a simple concept to enact and understand.

Most people do not want to fall victim to others, especially if those people are enemies or people they dislike. Such would be the ultimate betrayal of the self, reflecting the sentiment Benjamin N. Cardozo expressed when he said, "Justice is not to be taken by storm; she is to be wooed by slow advances." A quote like this can be very dangerous if used differently: 'Treachery is not to be employed swiftly; it is to be planned with methodical care.' This would Present a new respect for the notion of 'To kill quietly and with patience.' – T.C. Monk

Treachery is a childish and callous endeavor, often justified by those who engage in it as a means to eliminate the opposition before they have a chance to devise any preemptive measures of their own. This would make it a simple matter of self-preservation —a premeditated safety measure to ensure survival. But no matter the reason one might contrive for its usage, it still does not excuse the fact that it is a loathsome and debasing quality one should never employ.

I am sorry to say that there are no particular methods or telltale signs for recognizing Treachery in others. It is not a perceivable affectation, such as a quirky personality trait or a specific scent. Still, it remains an indiscernible characteristic that one keeps veiled until the Time comes to set it in motion, or it is exposed by their actions or someone else's. However, I would suggest that the best method one might use to familiarize oneself with the signs of Treachery in others may be found in the following list of practices:

1) Consider prior knowledge of such acts.

2) Use proper judgment toward others.

3) Prevent oneself from being placed in unfavorable situations.

4) Be sure to plan for every eventuality that can be thought of.

5) Do not engage in poor values or questionable business practices.

6) Demand the same quality and performance that you proffer to others.

The essence is the same whether it occurs in a game or real-life engagements. "The visible is a shadow cast by the invisible." – (Plato)

– LOVE –

(24)

The word "Love" is a noun. It refers to a deep affection or fondness for another person (or oneself), such as having a sweetheart or beloved, feeling a strong sense of care, or enjoying and cherishing something more than anything else. [Love has many other meanings, but its core is captured by the descriptions above.]

* * *

L.O.V.E. 'Links of Varied Elements.' What a name! I wonder who coined the term Love and why. I am uncertain of its true origin, but I am convinced that the anagram I contrived above fits the overall concept better than I expected. I also fashioned an acronym, 'Loyalty Oblation Volition Endowment.' I'm not sure why I chose to create anagrams and acronyms for words that have specific meanings in Life, but I'm glad I started, as I've come up with some doozies that speak more than their translations.

At first, I was petrified about what I would script for this piece. Not because of its complex and variable nature, but because I would be opening myself up to uncensored ridicule as I attempted to define it for others to ponder. This is especially true if I fail to include what others think should have been incorporated into this work, or if my interpretation does not align with their idealized view of it; in that case, I would kindly respond, "Write your own book!" I do understand that I cannot please everyone, nor will I attempt to; however, I am willing to go out on a limb and expose my soft underbelly. I intend to hopefully muscle through it with minimal injury to my self-esteem, despite attacking Love in its naked form.

In the face of growing timidity, and without a second thought for my tender ego, I put on my big boy pants and plunged headlong into the breach. I will endeavor to do this concept justice, or at least attempt to meet the readers' idyllic expectations regarding the knowledge of Love they seek, a more profound definition of and answers thereto, especially for those who may have been afraid to ask for clarity on the subject. I know how that feels, having been too reluctant to seek advice on Love, either because most people were failing miserably at it or because I didn't want to expose my own ignorance. Even though I managed to decipher the enigma of Love on my own, in part, I now hold tremendous respect and appreciation for its multiphasic essence.

Let us peer into the looking glass and see what treasures we can discover in its reflection.

The experience of Love varies from person to person, depending on how strongly one responds to the sense they receive from another or how they feel toward that person, whether real or imagined. Despite what one does, sometimes the substance of Love can manifest in a single glance, an absent touch, and quickly grow from there. At other Times, it is nurtured by charm, charisma, or any other beneficial aspect offered by its favor. There is no proper manner in which Love is perceived or adopted in one's Life. It is an aspect we all strive to perfect in our lives, yet we often falter when applying or accepting it in any form.

Love is an essence; humanity does not truly understand how it affects their nature or how it causes them to react. The difficulty lies in preparing for its mercurial constitution, as humanity is not its master but a slave to its prodigious nature. Although most have come to understand that it is not merely an influential and overwhelming emotional sensation from which they cannot escape, but rather a mercurial essence that elicits unpredictable reactions. Believe it or not, "Love is a sentimental attachment, an affectation of necessary sacrifice and indulgence." – T.C. Monk

There are several interchangeable sides to the prospect of Love, and each has its own shine and shadow encompassing it. Most people have a workable idea of what Love is and how it should feel, yet they lack the proper understanding of how to nurture and groom it for Future development. It takes patience, dedication, and determination to succeed in the game of Love. And yes, I said "game" for the simple reason that when one engages in it, one is gambling with one's emotions and well-being. Love is an expensive bet, and Life will not waive the ante.

Love is not just a presence of mind but a state of being that one must exist within. One should be fully aware of its delicate, mercurial nature and how it can change on a dime. It is a tenuous balancing act at every turn, especially when a recipient's needs exceed what they provide to another. This can sometimes create relationship problems, particularly if one individual's needs outweigh the other's efforts or willingness to give more than they are willing to.

When it comes to Love's essence, it can often create a powerful effect within one's mind and body, a measure that most frequently confuses and frustrates one to the point of mania. Whether it is a positive or a negative feeling generated within, it remains a problem we all struggle to solve, or at least an amenable prospect we can attempt to manage. I say 'manage' tentatively, as it takes practice, fortitude, and diligence to maintain its delicate balance of power, profit, access, and accountability.

Unfortunately, most people become so caught up in the beneficial feelings of Love that they often forget the pain and damage it can cause to their mental state when they are severed from its benevolent touch. It is a harsh reality for one to experience, and most people tend to lose themselves in its turbulent wake. However, if one can weather the storm, they will most likely emerge from it a bit jaded, if not somewhat worse for wear. The beneficial aspect of such an affliction is that it will quickly teach us that nothing good lasts forever, particularly without struggle.

The fervor of Love is not usually beholden to one particular impression or another. It is most likely related to either a collection of sensory stimulants exuded by others or something experienced solely by the affected. Although another's imagination sometimes feels its heat, it can, unintentionally, unbeknownst to the person of interest, begin to foster in them. These illusory relationships are assumed or implied in these circumstances by a single look or innocent smile, some misinterpreted gesture, or just because one's mind fancies them.

I am guilty of this indulgence (like most other humans), as I have had a heart-wrenching desire for Jennifer Love Hewitt for most of my Life. It is not based on a look, a gesture, or any comment she made to me personally, but just how my mind wove its desire for a bellibone person like her. And even though I understood my mind manufactured its Eide, I realized it was not something shared between two people for mutual benefit. Its essence has remained in my mind for decades, and just having the yearning it wove for her taught me how to Love someone from afar, without a need to voice it or physically touch her, except within the numerous scenarios among the haven of my mind—a safe place for both of us to exist. (Hopefully, I wrote this tastefully.)

However, for the most part, the stirrings of Love are amicable for all parties involved. Most humans wish to feel loved by someone or to Love something. It is in our genes. Its sense veritably enamors us and makes us jealous of others who readily enjoy it without us. I have felt this way several Times while watching a group of people enjoying their connections with one another, but such is the benefit and gift of Love. It is to be shared and enjoyed by those who not only offer it but also accept it from others, as no one can appreciate what they do not participate in.

In our contrived reality, Love is harmony, pleasure, pain, and Despair. It can be one's saving grace while simultaneously existing as a double-edged sword that can cut both its victim and wielder with the same effect. Three quotes define the temperamental side of Love in its most genitive forms. The first is, "The art of pleasing consists of being pleased." – (William Hazlitt). The second is, "Suffering is permanent, obscure, and dark, and shares the nature of infinity." – (Wordsworth). The third is, "There is no Despair so absolute as that which comes with the first moments of our first great sorrow." – (George Eliot).

The engagement of Love -overall - is an ever-shifting kaleidoscope of emotional investment and sacrifice. It does not easily share the nature of its essence, nor will it allow one to master its domain. Such is a strange concept to accept, especially since the mind of another human being contrived the word itself (like any other). So, why does humanity spend so much Time and energy attempting to define Love and how it should be? Yet, it still manages to confound us despite being a simple four-letter word meant to instill kindness and unity.

It is quite a conundrum. However, I am sure we all place more emphasis on it than it was initially intended to carry. But this is the beauty of language, knowledge, the art of creative expression, and progressive thinking. Most things in Life have a mutable composition, no matter the origin of their creation, and like humans, they are ever-shifting. With the prospect of change comes new Life, which in turn begets the freedom to choose another path and create something tangible from the streams of Time, the amorphous shroud of Eternity, and the unstructured nature of existence.

It is said that Love is the one essence of creation that we humans will do anything to obtain. It is the quintessential product of emotional participation with another sentient Life form. It can sometimes express its quiddity without the need or presence of words. To be in Love with or have Love for something or someone else (Jessica Alba) does not express a sense of weakness, timidity, or surrender, but rather the presence of care, concern, and the ability to compromise with another. Samuel Coleridge said this poignantly when he wrote, "No voice, but oh! the silence sank like music on my heart."

The concept above encompasses one's intentions toward a specific person or thing, surpassing all others. It also denotes that one has a quantifiable measure of attraction, devotion, and conviction to support this particular Life or essence. All of us would like to think that Love can be measured in weight, distance, or degrees, but that is not the case, as Love is not a tangible thing that can be weighed or defined by worldly standards of measurement. It is an essence that can only be calculated by the human heart, for it is the one true gauge of all things humanly connected, such as what humanity has Love for, gives Love to, or receives it from. Nothing else in the world can do this.

The measure of Love humans have for one another can (and does) change over Time. It depends on how we treat one another on a daily basis. However, this can change sharply when one's progeny becomes part of the equation. And, just because a person has offspring does not diminish the Love they have cultivated with their significant other. It dramatically shifts its quality of importance and protection into an alternate pattern of applicability. One's significant other does not lose the Love they harbor for them, but it is repositioned and applied to another part of what they (together) created.

These individuals (the parents) are no longer as crucial to each other as they once were. Their creation now becomes the object of their affection and Love, and tends to be what both will sacrifice everything for, ensuring it survives and brings forth another like itself through Love. However, humanity's handicap in how long Love can affect them truly reveals its depth of innocence. Most people do not realize how profoundly it can influence one's personality, Life, the lives of others, and any engagements they participate in. It is not that humans are stupid, blind, or inept to such matters of companionship and trust, but they have yet to truly grasp the profundity of Love's intrinsic nature.

Love has a tenor that we all feel and experience in myriad ways, and it affects each of us at different times. How we allow it to affect us is entirely based on how much Time and effort we invest in it. Nothing good is easy, and anything worth experiencing should have a modicum of challenge to it, or what sense is there in chancing the wheel of Fate? Why gamble if there is no reward for which one risks or invests in the contest for gain? Everyone should be willing to risk what they have to acquire what they want, or what use is there in playing the game of Life? Nothing good can come from a useless endeavor.

I would posit that as a society and a race of beings, we all desire more than we have, and it is our responsibility to work towards preserving the blessings that grace has bestowed upon us. And when it comes to Love, we all seek that elusive charm to bestow its blessings not only on our existence but also on the lives we care for, fight for, and sacrifice to protect, in the Hope of achieving such longevity. As sentient beings, employing such a measure is within our purview. Still, it must be genuine, motivated by altruistic intent, and not used to pursue personal gain at another's expense. Ultimately, Love is our home, world, and the essence of all Life. If you find fault, please enlighten me with your interpretation of what Life and Love genuinely are.

In conclusion, I felt it pertinent to include the following quotes, hoping they would not only shed a bit more light on the subject but also offer something to ponder before moving on.

"The course of true Love never did run smooth." – (Shakespeare)

"The magic of first Love is our ignorance that it can never end." – (Moliere)

"Love is merely a guiding light to the heart of another." – T.C. Monk

"I wonder if my first Love loved me first." (Paraphrased from 'Hillsong Young and Free')

No quotes better express or sum up such sentiments. These statements remain true today and have a profound impact on every human being, unapologetically.

– HATE –

(25)

The word "Hate" is a noun. It is defined as an intense dislike, antipathy, or loathing toward a person, place, thing, idea, or feeling.

* * *

Hate is a learned trait, not an innate quality or natural inclination. It is an incivility humanity has become infected with, one that is not only based on other people's biases (their preferential aversions) but also on the same influential and bigoted egotisms they find exhibited in their surroundings. Those who engage in such behavior do so out of Fear of being ostracized by their peers or family, rather than out of any Hatred they have developed toward anyone else or any shame or disparagement they have endured at another's expense. No beneficial or positive attributes can be ascribed to Hate, nor can any good come from applying it in any fashion.

During my troubled and imperfectly balanced Life, I have engaged in many forms of Hate-mongering, which I am confident is echoed by 98 percent of the world in one form or another. No one is entirely exempt from such conduct, as all of humanity suffers from some form of bias, bigotry, and Hate in all they do. Be it religion, politics, money, gender, social status, identity, or some form of disability, it is a form of bias and oppressive thinking. Such a predisposition is not based on predominant genetics, but rather on a selective nature, a mutual inclination where they can either be in concert with others who share the same desires, like-minded interconnectivity, or engage with those who share the same disposition for self-imposed separatism and/or preferential omission.

Most humans misunderstand the true nature of Hate and bandy the word around to describe all things they either despise or can do without. This is not the nature of Hate, but more so the constitution of disdain. For those who lack a clear understanding of the definition of Hate, most tend to label it with Catholic terminology, one encompassing all things they either do not wish to habituate or desire to have excised from their Life. This brings to mind two quotes: "Men Love in haste, but they detest at leisure" – (Lord Byron), and "Hate is the presence of moral objection, a sense of righteous indignation." – T.C. Monk

As I mentioned in a previous paragraph, my engagement with Hate has been extensive. This was not something my parents taught me through their actions (except for their own experiences with a particular person or class), but rather a personal objection, peripheral disdain, and vocal characterizations shaped by others. It was not based on one person's design but contrived by the actions of all those around me, developed through my observations of an individual's deportment. Learning how different cultures interact with those outside their own can be significantly different from what one hears from others versus what one perceives for oneself.

It is a shame how abhorrent and disgraceful some humans treat one another, especially when one ascribes to the maxim, "Do unto others before they do unto you." – (Terry Pratchett). It is said that 'hurt people, hurt people.' Such an engagement is quite the opposite, not only with strangers but also with loved ones. Why anyone would ever wish to abuse or hurt anyone else - unless it is an activity involving a Vice - I cannot honestly explain other than to say it is a Choice to inflict pain or injury upon another, especially a loved one, over a stranger. I believe this is because the offender assumes they have a better chance of being forgiven for trespassing against a friend or family member than against an outsider. Erich Segal's sentiment resonates deeply here. "Love means never having to say you're sorry."

The fey notion most humans do not consider regarding Hate is the fact that its essence often stems from - believe it or not - Love and covetousness. Now, I know most readers might haughtily disagree with this assertion, perhaps even balk at such a ludicrous statement, but it is an absolute truth. The concept of this school of thought centers on an aversion to or attraction to a particular thing or idea. Such a feeling may indicate that (at some point in Time) this person must have loved it or coveted the essence it exposed them to, only to detest it. One does not simply Hate out of a purely autonomous or desire-based impulse. They must have initially developed some feelings for it, for one to Hate now what they once had an emotional connection to, or for

However, if the above definition still does not sway your thinking, consider it in another form. "The Hate one gives or feels would be a direct result of either the loss they feel by its absence, being restricted from its presence, or the sickness they are plagued by due to its unwanted presence in their immediate vicinity." – T.C. Monk. It is completely unnatural for the human heart to Hate for any reason. Its veritable disposition is benevolent and designed to feel and express compassion, sympathy, friendship, kindness, and empathy toward all Life. It was never meant to inflict pain or harm upon another or itself, as its primary function in Life is to care for its host until it gives out.

There is no argument against self-evident truths, as such concepts should be easy to grasp, discern, or understand. One should consider this the next Time they encounter something they desire or need. Consider how the heart feels after seeing or experiencing it. Does it evoke feelings of happiness, joy, or envy, or does it instill a strong desire to possess it with an aggressive nature? William Hazlitt intimated something regarding the dichotomy of Love and Hate when he wrote, "Violent antipathies are always suspicious and betray a secret affinity."

I completely agree with this axiom, as its practice is rampant in human society today and has been for untold years. Most girls are exposed to this type of behavior at a young age, primarily when they are picked on by a boy who secretly fancies them, often during coed interactions at school.

Consider this: what if one were to experience it in a different format, something that affects them physically and emotionally, such as animal magnetism (Also Known as Love at first sight)? Would one do anything to obtain its measure? Would one be willing to sacrifice everything to acquire it for oneself? Would one consider any act as being justified in safeguarding its essence? Does its protection complement the partisan beneficially? Would one be willing to proffer their own Life to defend its Future existence? And would its substance profit the giver enough to either equal or outstrip the price they are willing to commit as remuneration?

These queries will not only make or break one's involvement with its quiddity but weave the threads of Hate and discontent within those jealous of another's devotion to it. The nature of such relative factors serves as evidence of the dynamic proximity of Love and Hate. The immolations in the actuation of each prove how they are not only intimately intertwined, but the substance of each notion is imbued with equal vigor. It is not necessarily a bad thing, but an existential reality of Life in general. Humans cannot have one without the other, as it would not provide a tangible basis for comparison. An absence like this would prevent one from experiencing any essence, whether positive or negative, in design.

Now, if the latter portion of this concept is a bit difficult to grasp in the current sense, consider it in the following manner. How does one feel when they breathe? Is there any particular feeling other than drawing breath? Are there any emotions, sensations, or physical elements that affect a person? No, there is not. The only Time one will feel anything for the substance of air, or the desire to breathe, is when the ability to do so is lost. The implication here is that its essence is subjective and influenced by one's surroundings, rather than a hereditary trait passed down from birth.

There is no such thing as an inborn characteristic that naturally develops the idiosyncrasy of Hate. As they mature, they cultivate an affectation shaped by the influences around them. Instead, these influences manifest through what they hear from their parents, siblings, friends, the internet, and television, and through what they observe in their environment; all of this directly shapes the bias in the minds of everyone exposed to it. To paraphrase Einstein, "Hate is nothing more than a deposit of prejudices laid down in the mind before you reach eighteen."

However, according to Willa Cather, there is such a thing as 'Creative Hate. This notion is not only a manifestation of grand proportion but can verily harm everyone it touches. It does not matter where it stems or where it occurs, but it is a malignancy on the backside of the world. 'Creative Hate' is much like a chameleon, adept at using deception to disguise itself. However, it can strike like a deadly asp from out of nowhere. Nothing in Life is more dangerous or compelling than its practice, as it is an intentional and evil contrivance by design. The power of its sway is malignant, and its quiddity can be derived from the following relative quotes:

"A falsehood created by Hate told enough Times, will one day become an assumed fact - a truth of its own." – T.C. Monk

"I detest that man who hides one thing in the depths of his heart and speaks from another." – (Shakespeare)

"A truth that's told with false intent beats all the lies you can invent." – (William Blake)

"Hate manifests in the mind of the despised, in those who are hateful, in the sick, and the envious." – T.C. Monk

"I want that glib and oily art to speak and purpose not." – (Shakespeare)

"Don't be fooled by the touch of goodness in evil's hands, for the seeds of turpitude flourish among the best of flowers." – T.C. Monk

The profound nature and intent woven within the above quotes prove that its practice has been (and still is) rampant in human society and that most humans engage in it more than they should. Most would call it slander; some tag it as deceit, while others might define it as fraudulent. Regardless of what moniker it carries, it is simply character assassination and moral turpitude, both of which are practices relied upon by the weak, the confused, violent cowards who Fear the consequences of the truth, and those who have no self-respect.

Having spent the better part of my Life behind bars, I have learned a great deal about the sickness of Hate and its malicious influence. Having been surrounded by its toxic essence daily, I am confident enough to dub its negative comportment as 'The skin of evil.' I tag it in such a manner to identify not only those who use it with absolute malice but also those with no remorse who choose to malign or bear false witness against them. Such a pursuit is dangerous because it can become all-consuming, destroying its intended target and harming everyone around it, including the user.

Hate has a diverse and intense nature that magnifies one's sense of desire and enhances one's sadistic tendencies, intensifying the perverse pleasure it can bring, especially at another's expense. Hate should be one of those contrivances we, as sentient beings, completely excise from the ethos of our entire species with prejudice. Nothing of its malignant nature has any moral or redeeming value for anyone but the malicious, the hateful, and the corrupt.

Epilogue

And the end is here! What a fantastic, mind-bending journey this has been for me. I am quite relieved to have completed this artistic rendition, and I hope readers have enjoyed a peek behind the veil of my mind. There is no better feeling in the world for a writer than finishing a work meant for mass consumption. It is a pleasure to look back on it and wonder, 'Where did all of this come from?' 'How did I fashion this into a manuscript I could share with the world?' 'Was it always present in my mind, like a statue inside a stone?'

One can only wonder about its theory of contrivance, but wherever it originated, be it the depths of my mind or the unknown expanse of the universe, I am humbled either way and very grateful to have been graced with such joy in my Life. Not many people can say that Time has simultaneously allowed them to reflect on their importance and their insignificance. I had not thought it possible to grasp such a dichotomy in this way, but I stand corrected in my ignorance and wish the same for others who desire such illumination in their lives.

With the completion of this collective work, I am satisfied that what I have included herein may help others not only gather a sense of the things around them and how each of them connects us in a more existential sense, but also an Aire of someone they have never even met and may someday wish to. It is rare for one in my position to have the drive to accomplish something of this magnitude, given the environment I inhabit, which is filled with Hate, Doubt, Vice, Treachery, Deceit, Nightmares, and Death. Despite these dour concepts being ever-present around me, I have not lost Faith that, with dedication and determination, the concepts of Hope, Dreams, Eternity, Choice, Life, Virtue, and the Future hold great promise for those who seek their undiscovered blessing.

At this stage, I want all my readers to understand that the concepts we ascribe to, attempt to follow, or infuse into our lives are not etched in stone. Such notions are malleable and ever-changing as we trudge along the road of Life. No concept, idea, or aspect will ever be the same for anyone. We all have our desires about how we would like such matters to affect our personal development and our interactions with others. But what we want and receive are often two different things.

As frustrating as this might be for some folks, I think such conflicting measures are necessary for Life so that one does not become complacent with the ease with which things come to them or with a structure that does not challenge them. This understanding came to me when I realized that most people in modern society have grown accustomed to relying on others rather than working for themselves. Most people would fail on their own merits if forced to rely solely on their skills to survive in the wild, let alone thrive in adversity.

Most have lost their innate hunter-gatherer nature due to the rapid pace of modern life. The individual's desire to fend for oneself has been stifled, devalued, and made obsolete in most countries bent on corporate monopolies and the slave labor of the masses. Everyone who has a job, whether working for someone or oneself, is part of the world's slave labor force. We all work for someone. Whether in the typical workforce or as an individual creating items for sale, we work for those who consume what we make, create, or provide for essential use and the comfort of life.

I am not saying there is anything wrong with being part of the massive workforce that drives the engine of our world, nor am I deprecating those who choose to work individually for personal or communal goals. I am simply noting that we all toil for someone else, which is, at its core, slave labor. Everyone who works gets paid, and the payment is always made by someone else for the work they provide. It is simply the way of the world, and nothing is wrong with it. One needs clarification to recognize one's reality and not scoff at those who reveal the truth of its design.

That said, I will close this out with a final thought. The standards of measure we all seek to glean from Life are no different from the concepts that preceded us, ones forged by those who carved the roads we now trudge. Granted, such paths are much easier now that others have smoothed out the rough edges for us, but we all need to be more aware that the society we live in is not a perpetual state guaranteed to anyone. Once it begins to crumble and its structure dissolves before our eyes, we will again be forced to relearn the skills to keep us alive and provide for those we Love.

Thank you all for your Time and dedication to this work. It is humbling to realize that someone else not only desires to know what is on another's mind but also to take it on and apply it to their own life. It is a fantastic feeling to have put my name out in the world, along with my knowledge and the legacy of my family name. At least my whole life was not a waste of time and air that someone else could have put to better use.

To all the scions of the stars, I say, "Stay humble, be blessed, and feel divine. There is no other way to be."

Glossary

The terms defined below do not encompass the full definition of the word used, but only the pertinent parts that apply to the particular place they are found in this work.

Acumen - Keen insight or discernment.

Aggregate - The total amount gathered or combined into one whole.

Allusion - A reference, especially a subtle, passing, or indirect one.

Amorphous - Shapeless, vague, and unstructured.

Antipathy - A firm or deep-rooted dislike or aversion.

Aplomb - Confidence, self-assurance.

Apropos - Relevant, appropriate, or concerning.

Arrant - Utter, outright.

Asceticism - A lifestyle of severe self-discipline and abstention from all pleasures.

Augury - An omen, portent, prophecy, or interpretation of signs.

Autogenous - Self-produced or self-generated.

Avarice - Excessive greed for wealth or possessions.

Bellibone - A woman who excels in both beauty and virtue.

Bourgeois - Conventional, dull, and materialistic.

Cede - To relinquish rights or possessions.

Chimera - A fantastical or grotesque creation of the imagination.

Chimerical - Imaginary or unreal.

Confluence - Coming together.

Connote - Implied in addition to the literal or primary meaning.

Contretemps - An awkward or unfortunate occurrence.

Copious - Abundant, plentiful.

Corollary - A natural consequence.

Crescendoed - Increased gradually in loudness or intensity.

Daedal - Complex, intricate, and skillful.

Delineate - To portray by drawing or in words.

Demarcation - Marking a boundary or limit.
Deportment - Behavior or manners.
Despondent - In low spirits, dejected.
Dichotomy - Division into two, especially a sharply defined one.
Dint - By force or means of.
Disputation - Debating, arguing, controversy, formal debate.
Ecumenical - Universal.
Eide - Of Eidos.
Eidos - plural: Eide - an essence.
Eking - Struggling to make a living or support an existence.
Eldritch - Weird.
Empirical - Based on observation or experiment, not theory.
Equitable - Fair, just.
Festooning - Decorating elaborately.
Fey - Strange, otherworldly, whimsical.
Fictive - Imaginary.
Foist - To impose.
Flippancy - Frivolousness, levity, lightheartedness, disrespect.
Flurch - A multitude, many, spoken of things, not persons.
Fractals - A geometric pattern repeated at an increasingly smaller scale to create irregular shapes that classical geometry cannot depict. Broken, uneven.
Futurist - A believer in human progress, a student of the future.
Gamut - An entire series, range, or scope of anything.
Genitive - Close association or possession.
Hubris - Overbearing pride.
Ideation - The act of forming an idea.
Ideating - The process of creating an idea.
Ignoble - Dishonorable, mean.
Illations - The act or process of inferring or drawing conclusions. A conclusion: deduction.
Immolation - Killing or offering as a sacrifice.
Impetus - A driving force or impulse, the force or energy with which a body moves.
Impious - Wicked, profane.
Incertitude - Uncertainty, doubtfulness, doubt.

THE TIES THAT BIND

Inotropic - Affecting muscular contractility.
Inquietude - Uneasiness.
Interstice - An intervening space, chink, or crevice.
Insouciantly - Carelessly, heedlessly, indifferently, unconcernedly.
Kinetic - Related to motion.
Limpid - Clear, transparent.
Literati - Learned people.
Mediocrity - Second-rate, of middling quality.
Menagerie - Small zoo.
Mercurial - Characterized by changing moods quickly; often regarded as changeable, lively, and quick.
Mettle - Strength of character, spirit, courage.
Mewling - Crying feebly, whimpering.
Modicum - Small amount.
Nonpareil - Unmatched, unique.
Oblation - An offering to a divine being; a prayer.
Omnipotent - Having great or absolute power and significant influence.
Omnispective - Capable of seeing everything; beholding all things.
Orphic - Mystical.
Ostentatious - Showy, boastful, pretentious, theatrical.
Overlet - To let in excess.
Paradigm - An example or pattern.
Paradoxical - a statement that is self-contradictory or fundamentally absurd, even if it is well-supported. It also refers to a person or thing that possesses conflicting qualities.
Paragon - Model of excellence.
Passim - To be found in various places throughout the text, here and there, everywhere.
Pedagogical - Meant to instruct or teach.
Pernicious - Destructive, ruinous, deadly.
Philter - Love potion, or to put someone under the spell of such.
Piddling - Trivial, insignificant.
Pragmatic - Dealing with matters based on practical requirements or consequences.
Prescient - Having foreknowledge or foresight.
Privity - Private knowledge.

Privy - Sharing in the secret of something hidden.
Prodigious - Marvelous or astonishing, enormous.
Propinquity - Nearness in space, proximity, close kinship, similarity.
Propitious - Favorable, advantageous.
Pulchritude - Beauty.
Quiddity - The essential nature of a thing; a trivial difference; an essence; an unreasonably fine distinction or quibble.
Rectitude - Moral uprightness, correctness.
Reformative - Having the quality of renewing or reforming.
Remuneration - recounting.
Replete - Filled or well-supplied; teeming.
Scions - Descendants.
Scoff - Speak derisively, mock, or be scornful; mocking words or taunts.
Sodalities - Societies.
Somatology - The science or doctrine of the general properties of material substances, particularly somatic ones.
Specious - Appearing plausible but actually wrong.
Stultified - Made ineffective, useless, or futile, mainly due to routine.
Suasion - Persuasion used instead of force.
Sylvan - Of the woods; wooded or rural.
Telescopic - Compressed in space or time.
Temporal - Related to time; temporary.
Threnody - A song of lamentation or mourning.
Tour de force - A feat of strength or skill.
Trenchant - Incisive, terse, and vigorous.
Transcendental – Going beyond experience; not based on it.
Unctuous - Oily; having a greasy or soapy feel.
Undulated - Moving in a wavy motion.
Volition - The exercise of the will; the power of willing.
Widdershins - (variation of withershins), moving in the opposite direction.

✳ ▼ ✳

– Words used in this work have come from multiple dictionaries over the past 40+ years. I cannot tag each reference book here because I do not remember the exact names of all the books I consulted. I credit the definitions included herein not only for the reader's benefit but also to acknowledge the companies that published the referenced books. –

Author Bio

T.C. monk is an artist who excels across multiple media. His talents are self-taught and have been refined during a lengthy prison sentence. While incarcerated, he has dedicated much of his time to studying prose, poetry, ink-and-pencil art, history, ethics, language, philosophy, psychology, theology, and the interconnectedness of family and relationships.

Courtesy, honesty, fidelity, trust, respect, honor, patience, hospitality, perseverance, and sacrifice are traits he has worked to instill in himself, hoping not only to build something from a broken existence but also to prove that with dedication, discipline, and determination, anyone can change their life for the better; all they need to do is try.

Being in prison did not teach him anything valuable because the system is fundamentally flawed and not designed for teaching, correction, or rehabilitation. It is primarily a place to warehouse people, allowing the prison industry to profit from their sweat and labor. He believes that going to prison may have saved his life and given him a chance to dedicate himself to creating something better. He realized that people could either use their time to benefit themselves or, like many others in prison, waste away... never leaving their mark on the world.

Direct messaging with the author is available by email at www.securustech.net[1] (including the inmate's name and ID #) or by snail mail to the Arizona Department of Corrections, Rehabilitation and Reentry, Timothy C. Monk, ADCRR #068675, Eyman Complex/Browning Unit, P.O. Box 211309, Dallas, Texas 75211.

---

1.   http://www.securustech.net

Don't miss out!

Visit the website below and you can sign up to receive emails whenever T.C. Monk publishes a new book. There's no charge and no obligation.

https://books2read.com/r/B-A-TGZAB-ITXRC

BOOKS2READ

Connecting independent readers to independent writers.